Hidden Sayings of Jesus

Hidden Sayings of Jesus

Words attributed to Jesus
outside the Four Gospels

William G. Morrice

HENDRICKSON
PUBLISHERS

To Katharine
as we approach our ruby wedding anniversary
and in memory of our parents
from whom we first heard sayings of Jesus

Hendrickson Publishers, Inc.
PO Box 3473
Peabody Massachusetts 01961–3473

First published in Great Britain 1997
SPCK
Holy Trinity Church
Marylebone Road
London NW1 4DU

ISBN: 1–56563–289–3

Printed in Great Britain

Contents

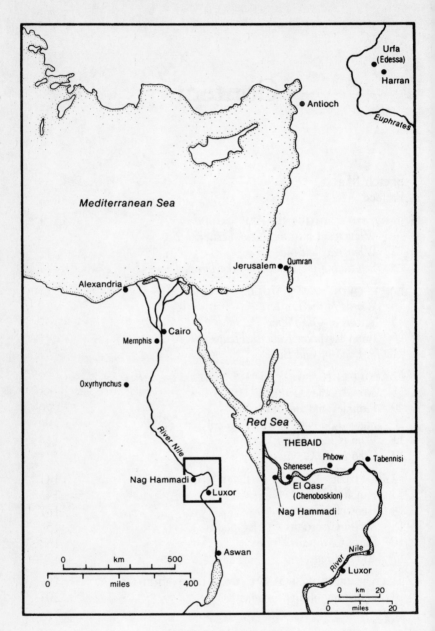

SKETCH MAP

showing Oxyrhynchus (**6.1**); Chenoboskion (**7.1**);
Nag Hammadi (**7.2**); Alexandria (**7.4**); Edessa (**8.10–17**)

Preface

For many years, I have been interested in the *agrapha* – sayings of Jesus not written in the four gospels. As a Scottish divinity student, I acquired secondhand copies of James Hope Moulton's *From Egyptian Rubbish Heaps* and George Milligan's *Here and There among the Papyri*. Some thirty years ago, while still a parish minister, I was asked a question about the *Gospel of Thomas*, to which I probably gave a rather unsatisfactory reply. Soon after my change from parish ministry to college lecturing, my attention was again drawn to this apocryphal gospel by a German layman. So when the opportunity came of prolonged research by regular academic sabbaticals, I turned with relish to the learning of Coptic and to systematic delving into the Coptic *Gospel of Thomas*, the largest existing depository of these unwritten sayings. There, amongst the dross of encratism, I discovered hidden treasure.

I have been encouraged by the suggestion made to me by the Senior Editor of SPCK to gather together and translate other sayings of Jesus hidden outside the canonical gospels, to set them within the context of a discussion of the New Testament canon and to evaluate critically their authenticity. I have eagerly accepted this challenge in the hope that some of the labours of successive sabbaticals and early semi-retirement will be made available to a wider public than I had originally planned. The result is a fairly comprehensive, though not exhaustive, collection of sayings of Jesus outside the four gospels. Since the book has been written for a general readership without any background in academic theology, introductory chapters contain simple summaries rather than scholarly discussion, which has as far as possible been relegated to notes at the end. These can be ignored by those who do not wish to get involved in detailed study.

When dealing with individual sayings, I have tried to indicate how far each one is likely to be authentic – the most likely being graded A, where there is some doubt B, the more doubtful C, and the most doubtful D. Personal judgement is, of course, involved in such grading and others will differ in their assessment. A fuller explanation of my choice and of the tests that I have used in determining authenticity can be found at the end of chapter 3. Items included in suggestions for further reading will not only point to sources that I have used in the course of my research. They should also help those who wish to pursue further their own enquiries into any aspects of this fascinating subject.

With regard to the text of the sayings, two things require to be made clear. First, square brackets indicate suggested restorations of gaps in manuscripts and ellipses (. . .) show where individual letters or words are mutilated or illegible. Second, the English rendering is my own although I have consulted many translations, including various versions of the Bible. For the Arabic sayings I have translated from the Latin versions provided by Michael Asin.

I am most grateful to Rachel Boulding, Senior Editor, Catherine Mann and the rest of the staff at SPCK, including anonymous readers, all of whom have been very helpful in the long process of bringing this project to completion.

Finally, I wish to record my thanks to my wife, without whose constant help and support this book could not have been written. During the gradual process of retiring, she not only had to put up with my two part-time jobs but also with the ever-present distraction of a computer and its demands for attention from her husband.

William G. Morrice

The Cedars
Edinburgh

Part One

Digging for Gold

CHAPTER ONE

What went into the New Testament?

1 Like Topsy

In her novel, *Uncle Tom's Cabin*, Harriet Beecher Stowe tells us in chapter 20 about Topsy, the little eight-year-old slave-girl whom St Clare bought for his cousin. Miss Ophelia:

> 'Who was your mother?' Topsy was asked by her new mistress.
>
> 'Never had any mother!' said the little girl with a grin.
>
> Miss Ophelia was surprised. 'Never had any mother! What do you mean? Where were you born?'
>
> 'Never was born!' persisted Topsy with another grin.
>
> Somebody else asked her, 'Do you know who made you?'
>
> 'Nobody, as I knows on,' said the child with a short laugh.
>
> The idea appeared to amuse her considerably; for her eyes twinkled and she said, 'I 'spect I grow'd. Don't think nobody ever made me.'

Like Topsy, the New Testament was not born suddenly, all twenty-seven books bound neatly together as one volume. No one person or even one church council suddenly decided that these twenty-seven books, no more and no less, comprised the documents of the Christian faith. The collecting and sifting process was a long and complicated one. It lasted for a period of three-and-a-half centuries, from approximately AD 50 to approximately AD 400. To be more exact, it lasted from AD 49, when Paul wrote his first letter, to AD 397, when formal sanction was given at the Council of Carthage to the canon of the New Testament as we have it today.

2 The Canon of the New Testament

But what is meant by the canon of the New Testament? The Greek word *kanon* occurs as early as Homer and was probably related to *kanna* ('reed'), from which we get the English word 'cane'. There is also a Hebrew word *kaneh* ('stalk'). This is found in the Old Testament with the meaning of measuring-rod (Ezekiel 40.3, 5). The basic meaning of the Greek word *kanon* is any straight rod or bar, especially something used to keep something else straight. So it was the word used of a carpenter's or a mason's rule or line.

From this basic meaning, there sprang several figurative meanings. Written law was the rule for discerning right and wrong. In Aristotle's *Ethnics*, the good man is the canon and measure of the truth. Philosophers had their rules or codes of behaviour; for example, the Epicurean canon. Alexandrian scholars called the collections of old Greek authors canons or models of excellence or classics, as we would say today.

In the New Testament, the word occurs only four times and always in Paul. It denotes the sphere of action or influence of an apostle or missionary (2 Corinthians 10.13, 15, 16). It also denotes a rule or principle of conduct (Galatians 6.16). In the second century, it was used of an unwritten code of truth or rule of faith followed and believed by Christians.

From the marks on a ruler, the word came to mean 'a list' and was a synonym for *katalogos*, from which we get 'catalogue' in English. In the pre-Reformation Church, the canon of the Mass was the list of persons commemorated in it, both the living and the dead for whom prayers were said. To put a dead person on such a list was to canonize him or her, to declare that person to be a saint. From this metaphorical sense of the word meaning 'list' comes the sense in which we refer to the canon of the New Testament or the canon of the Old Testament.

The idea of authoritative lists of books is still with us today. It applies not only to works bearing the papal imprimatur ('Let it be printed') as containing sound catholic doctrine and suitable for reading by Roman Catholics. Outside the religious sphere, we have English classics, which would include the works of Shakespeare and the novels of such authors as Charles Dickens and Sir Walter Scott. In recent years, many books have been written to promote feminist thought and theology and to stress the important role of women in society and in the Church. In one college library, all such books have been gathered together in one section, whatever their classification numbers according to the Dewey system, in order to assist those who wish to do research on these issues. There has also been an upsurge of books written by Africans for Africans.

There is nothing particularly religious or theological about having a canon or authoritative list of books. What ought we to read? What should school children read in order to pass their examinations? What books by recognized authorities should students read before writing an essay on a particular subject? The canon of the New Testament is the list of books recognized by the Christian Church as being authoritative in matters of faith and life.

The word was first applied to the New Testament Scriptures, as far as we can tell, by Athanasius, Patriarch of Alexandria, in the second half of the fourth century (**7.4**). He declared that the *Shepherd of Hermas*, an allegorical work that has been referred to as the *Pilgrim's Progress* of the early Church, did not belong to the canon. In his thirty-ninth *Easter Letter* written in AD 367, he referred to the Scriptures as being in the process of being canonized or listed in contrast to the Apocrypha (hidden books). Thus, the word itself came into use in connection with the canon of the New Testament only in the fourth century, at least as far as written records show; but the idea of having an authoritative list of books regarded as Scripture is much older.

3 Circulation of Separate Books

By the end of the first century AD, all the books that were later to be included in the New Testament had been written, with the

5

probable exception of 2 Peter. These various documents were circulated in manuscript form on papyrus rolls (5.1). They were copied by scribes and collected by congregations and individuals along with many other documents of lesser value.

Over and over again in the second century, we find pieces of evidence that show that the idea of a canon was taking shape in the minds of people. The word 'gospel' was coming to be used of a written book. In the *Didache* (*Teaching of the Twelve Apostles*), we are told not to pray as the hypocrites but 'as the Lord commanded in his gospel' (*Didache* 8.2). There follows the Lord's Prayer as found in Matthew 6.9–13 with the instruction to pray thus three times a day. Again, in Justin Martyr's *Apology* (**16.4**), written between AD 151 and 163, there are references to memoirs made by the apostles, called gospels – probably the earliest known appearance in writing of gospels in the plural.

4 Motives at Work

But why was it necessary for there to be such a list at all? The idea was derived from Judaism, since the Hebrew books of what we now know as the Old Testament were, between AD 90 and 100, selected for use in Jewish worship (**2.1**). While Christians as well as Jews accepted the Jewish Scriptures, Christians in addition felt the need to have their own New Testament Scriptures to place alongside what they had come to regard as the Old Testament.

Even more important than this was the great authority that Christians attached to the words of the Lord (Acts 20.35 – 4.2; 1 Thessalonians 4.15 – 4.4) and to any writings that could be proved to have come from the apostles. Alongside such genuine documents, there were other Christian writings of dubious authority and value. Some of these are preserved in what we know as the Apocrypha of the New Testament. Others are referred to as the Pseudepigrapha (books written under assumed names). Some have been lost to the light of day or have only recently been restored to it, like the *Gospel of Thomas*. Which, if any, of these writings could be safely used by Christians? The Church was gradually compelled to decide which documents contained true Christian tradition.

There was also a desire to preserve the Church from false

teaching or wrong beliefs. Towards the end of the first century, some people were arguing that Jesus was not really a human being. He was a divine being, the Son of God, who only appeared to be a man. According to tradition, the apostle John almost had an encounter with a leading upholder of this view, whose name was Cerinthus. When he heard that this heretic was in the public baths, John refused to enter in case the roof should fall on such an enemy of the truth. His doctrine was known as docetism, from the Greek verb *dokein* ('to appear'). Compare the views of Marcion in the middle of the second century (**1.7**).

One of the main heresies (false teachings) to arise in the second century was known as gnosticism, from the Greek word *gnosis* ('knowledge'). While Christian teaching as enunciated by Paul was that we are made right with God by God's grace, to which we respond in faith (Romans 3.23; 5.1), gnostics argued that communion with God depends upon knowledge. It is only those who understand the true mysteries of the faith who can be saved. This secret teaching had been entrusted by apostles to their favourite disciples. Gnostics circulated pseudonymous gospels, that is, gospels under assumed names, in support of their doctrine.

Another heresy arose in the second half of the second century, Montanism. This claimed that the age of revelation was not over and that the prophets of Montanus, a converted priest of the Phrygian goddess Cybele, spoke with the authority of the original apostles. Associated with Montanus were two prophetesses, Priscilla and Maximilla. A characteristic of Montanist prophecy was that it was delivered in an ecstatic trance.

The best defence against all such heretical teaching was the setting up of a canon of Scripture. In this way, the Church decided which books should be read in public worship and which should not, which books contained authentic Christian doctrine and which did not.

5 Tests of Canonicity

In the actual choosing of the canon, two main tests seem to have been at work. First and foremost, if a book was being read regularly in public worship, it was more likely to be selected than

7

one that found no place in the liturgical usage of the Church. Such public lection would make it more certain that a book would be authorized as Scripture and continue to be read aloud in the course of Christian worship.

Furthermore, if it was believed that a particular book had come from one of the apostles or depended upon the authority of such an eye-witness, then this additional factor was sufficient to guarantee its inclusion within the canon authorized by the Church as a whole.

These two tests of canonicity – public lection and apostolicity – made sure that each book had something to say to the Church at large and that what it said originated from those to whom the revelation in Jesus Christ was actually given – the apostles, including Paul.

In connection with this whole process of the selection of books for the New Testament, early writers frequently quoted a saying attributed to Jesus: 'Become skilled money-changers' (extracts 16.12, 22; **18.21**).

6 Three Main Periods

At first, there were no official pronouncements either by the Church as an institution or by individuals. The process was one of gradual growth stretching over three-and-a-half centuries. Three main periods can be traced – a period of separate circulation and gradual gathering of books into two groups (AD 50 to 200), a period of sorting out or sifting (AD 200 to 325), and a period of authoritative pronouncements (AD 325 to 400).

7 First Period

During the first century-and-a-half (AD 50 to 200), books were circulated separately round various congregations. At the same time, they were gradually being gathered into two groups – gospels and letters written by apostles.

In the middle of the second century, Marcion, the arch-heretic of his day, made a distinction between the God of the Old Testament and the God of the New Testament. The former was the Creator of the universe, the *Demiurge* (Maker or Architect), a just and righteous God who was ignorant, harsh and rigorous. The God of the New Testament was the good God, whose nature is love. Marcion believed that Jesus only appeared to be a human being (1.4). His beliefs led to his choice of a New Testament canon for himself and his followers – Luke's Gospel (without the birth stories) and ten letters written by Paul. Since he did not have any love for the Jews, he cut out all references to them in the letter to the Romans. Tertullian (16.7) called this criticizing with a pen-knife.[1]

About AD 170, Tatian, a Syrian Christian (8.13), produced either in Greek or in Syriac the first unified account of the life and ministry of Jesus known as the *Diatessaron*. Using the canonical gospels and perhaps also the *Gospel of Thomas* (8.1), he composed a connected account of the life and teaching of Jesus.

Irenaeus, Bishop of Lyons from about AD 178 (16.5), quoted from at least twenty books of the New Testament.

The *Muratorian Canon* from about the same time – the first known record of documents deemed canonical by the church at Rome – contained four gospels, the Acts of the Apostles, thirteen letters of Paul (including 1 and 2 Timothy and Titus), two or three letters of John, Jude and Revelation – twenty-two or twenty-three of the twenty-seven books in our New Testament. There was also an *Apocalypse of Peter*, 'which some of our company will not have read in church'.

8 Second Period

During the third century and the first quarter of the fourth century (AD 200 to 325), there was a sorting out of the various books that were in dispute. Two scholars investigated their status and recorded the results of their research.

Origen (about AD 185 to about AD 254), the greatest biblical scholar of the early Church (16.9), divided books into two classes – those which were recognized everywhere and those that were disputed in certain churches. The following were recognized everywhere: four gospels, thirteen letters of Paul, 1 Peter, 1 John, Acts and Revelation (twenty-one books). In addition, Origen did not question the right of the letter to the Hebrews to a place in the canon, though with regard to authorship he declared, 'Who wrote it, God alone knows.'

Eusebius of Caesarea (AD 270 to 340) made a similar investigation. He divided books into three classes – recognized, disputed and spurious. Recognized books amounted to twenty-two that we find in our New Testament – four gospels, Acts, fourteen letters of Paul (including Hebrews), 1 Peter, 1 John, and 'if it seems good' Revelation. Disputed books were James, Jude, 2 Peter, 2 and 3 John, spurious books were the *Shepherd of Hermas*, the *Letter of Barnabas*, the *Didache*, the *Apocalypse of Peter*, the *Acts of Paul*. The canon of Eusebius is virtually ours, since the Greek Church did not maintain his careful distinction between 'recognized' and 'disputed'. The latter very soon became 'recognized'. Thereafter, there were only slight fluctuations in the canon.

9 Third Period

The third period in the growth of the canon (AD 325 onwards) was one of authoritative pronouncements by individuals and by church councils.

In AD 363, the Council of Laodicea listed twenty-six books as canonical (omitting Revelation).

In his thirty-ninth *Easter Letter* of AD 367, Athanasius of Alexandria (**7.4**) defined a canon of twenty-seven books that corresponds exactly with our New Testament, apart from the fact that the letters of James, Peter, John and Jude are placed immediately after Acts, as they are in all early manuscripts.

All that remained to be done was for church councils to make authoritative pronouncements. In AD 397, the Council of Carthage sanctioned this list in its entirety. Through the Latin Vulgate of Jerome, begun in AD 382, this canon soon became widespread. In AD 692, the Council of Constantinople confirmed the canon of the New Testament for both East and West.

10 Like Topsy but not Topsy-turvy

Three things can be said by way of summary about the whole process of the growth of the canon of the New Testament.[2]

1. It was gradual. It was 350 years before the canon finally emerged as we have it today. Like Topsy, nobody really made it. It just grew.

2. It was largely informal. Church councils played very little part in the process until the end. They merely ratified the common mind and good sense of the Christian Church.

3. It was a best-conserving process. It was by no means topsy-turvy. All that was most worthwhile was finally and irrevocably included within the New Covenant, as the New Testament should more properly be called. It contains the record of the new agreement between God and humanity – the story of how God sent his only Son into the world (John 3.16) as 'mediator of a new covenant' through his death on the cross (Hebrews 12.24).[3]

The canon of the New Testament has been closed. No further books can be added to it. Here we have the complete list of twenty-seven books that are authoritative for Christians in matters of faith and life.

CHAPTER TWO

What was left out?

1 Books left out of the Old Testament

By the end of the first century AD, Jewish scholars had decided which books should be included within their Scriptures and which should not (1.4). Many of those that were excluded were originally written in Greek rather than Hebrew and are to be found in the Septuagint, the translation from Hebrew into Greek of the Jewish Scriptures made for Greek-speaking Jews living in Egypt. The books that were eventually left out of what Christians know as the Old Testament came to be called the Apocrypha.

Roughly speaking, the Apocrypha is the excess of the Septuagint over the Hebrew Old Testament. Since the Septuagint was the Bible of the early Church, many early Christian writers quote from apocryphal books as though they were Scripture. In the fourth century, Jerome included them in his Latin version of the Bible, begun in AD 382 and known as the Vulgate. Yet Jerome recognized the distinction between Old Testament books in Hebrew that were canonical and the rest, to which he gave the designation apocryphal. Included within the Apocrypha are 1 and 2 Esdras, Tobit, Judith, the Wisdom of Solomon, Ecclesiasticus, Baruch, the Prayer of Manasseh and 1 and 2 Maccabees.

In the sixteenth century, Protestant leaders began to have doubts about these extra books, refusing to give to them the status of inspired Scripture. They recognized their historical value and their use as instruction in good living. No doctrine, however, was to be based upon them alone. Outside the Roman Catholic Church, they continue to be regarded with a certain amount of suspicion. In contrast, both the Council of Trent (1556) and the First Vatican Council (1870) insisted on their place in the canon of Scripture.

2 Books left out of the New Testament

Books excluded from the New Testament have, in modern times, come to be known as the New Testament Apocrypha. The designation of books as apocryphal was already familiar in connection with Jewish books that did not find a place in the Old Testament. Yet there is a similar ambiguity in the use of the term 'apocryphal' with regard to writings excluded from the New Testament as with those left out of the Old Testament. The word 'apocryphal' took on a derogatory meaning that is not necessarily inherent in the Greek word.

In the first instance, apocryphal books were secret books held specially precious, and so hidden away, by second-century heretics such as gnostics (1.4). Later, the term came to be applied to those books that were not to be read in church because they contained heretical material. Some of them did lay claim to apostolicity by means of pseudonymous titles such as the *Gospel of Peter*, the *Gospel of Thomas*, the *Apocalypse of Peter* or the *Acts of Paul*.

Apocryphal gospels, some of which may embody trustworthy oral tradition, include Jewish-Christian gospels – the *Gospel of the Nazaraeans* (15.2), the *Gospel of the Ebionites* (15.3) and the *Gospel of the Hebrews* (15.4). There is also a *Gospel of the Egyptians* (15.5) and gospels under the name of an apostle – the *Gospel of Peter* (14.2), the *Gospel of Philip* (14.5), the *Gospel of Thomas* (chapters 8 to 12), the *Gospel of Judas* and the *Gospel of Bartholomew*. These are apocryphal Acts, like those of Peter (14.4), Paul, John, Andrew and Thomas. Many of the apocryphal writings have clearly been influenced by heretical beliefs.

3 Apocryphal Sayings

For the purpose of this present book, the most important are the apocryphal gospels. Here we can expect to find words which may have been spoken by Jesus.

13

In the Preface to the Coptic *Gospel of Thomas*, we read: 'These are the hidden sayings which the living Jesus spoke and Didymus Judas Thomas wrote.' The Greek equivalent of the Coptic adjective translated here as 'hidden' would be *apokruphos* – 'hidden away'. This is used in the Greek translation of the Old Testament (the Septuagint – **2.1**) of what has been hidden and kept secret and will be revealed. Cyrus, for example, is told that God will give him dark treasures hidden away and open up for him unseen treasures in order that he may know that it is the God of Israel who is calling his name (Isaiah 45.3). In Mark 4.22 and in *Thomas* 5 (10.32; 6.13), a similar promise is made by Jesus about every cryptic thing (*krupton*) being revealed and every apocryphal thing (*apokrupton*) coming to light.

4 Greek Word

The Greek word *apokruphos* is made up of two parts – a preposition (*apo* – 'away from') and the root *krup* found also in the verb *kruptein* ('to hide'; compare English word 'crypt'). So *apokruptein* means to hide away something in order to prevent its being seen or found either because it is very precious or because it is objectionable. It is this alternative motivation that may account for the varying usage of the term both in Greek and in English.

Matthew sees in Jesus' use of parables in his teaching of the crowds the fulfilment of Psalm 78.2 – 'I will open my mouth in parables, I will proclaim what has been hidden since the foundation of the world' (Matthew 13.35). Matthew or his source has introduced the word 'hidden' (*kekrummena*[1]) into this quotation. In the Septuagint, the word is 'problems', translating a Hebrew term meaning 'riddles, enigmas, proverbs, parables'. For the psalmist, these perplexing problems from the past, enigmas of history, are lessons drawn from Israel's past. It is no mere narrative of fact that is recounted by the psalmist. Here is history that is full of significance for those who can penetrate its hidden meaning. No word for 'hidden' occurs in the Hebrew text. Matthew has read it into the Hebrew word for 'dark sayings'.

In Matthew 25.18, the servant to whom his master entrusted only one talent or bag of gold was so frightened of the responsibility that he dug a hole and hid (*ekrupsen*) his master's money in the ground for safe-keeping.

Paul declares that he speaks a wisdom of God hidden away (*apokekrummenen*) in secret, which God decreed before the ages for our glory (1 Corinthians 2.7). This wisdom he identifies with Christ (1 Corinthians 1.24, 30), in whom are hidden away (*apokruphoi*) all the treasures of wisdom and knowledge (Colossians 2.3).

It is clear that, in the New Testament as in the Old Testament, the word 'apocryphal', ('hidden away') does not have the derogatory significance that the English word often contains. Nevertheless, from the third century on, the Greek word was used as a technical term to denote books that should not be read in church.

However, the fact that 'the sayings of the living Jesus' are hidden away or apocryphal does not imply the hidden nature of gnostic doctrine which can be revealed only to those who have been initiated into the mysteries of gnosticism. The implication is simply that the teaching of Jesus can be understood by those who have faith and does not require any special knowledge. 'To you it has been given to know the mysteries of the kingdom of heaven, but to those it has not been given' (Matthew 13.11).

5 *Gospel of Thomas*

Of all the apocryphal books circulating in the early centuries, the most important for our present study is the Coptic *Gospel of Thomas*. This is the richest collection of sayings of Jesus outside the New Testament. It contains several that were hitherto unknown. Scholars have been divided as to which are authentic and which are not. As time goes by, more and more of the sayings may be regarded as going back to Jesus in some form or other.[2] The task of evaluating them will be undertaken in chapters 9 to 12.

6 Other Sources of Hidden Sayings

In addition to the New Testament Apocrypha, sayings of Jesus are found elsewhere. A few are found in some late manuscripts of the gospels (4.5–10) or in the New Testament outside the gospels

(4.1–4). Christian writers of the first four centuries such as Clement of Rome (**16.2**), Justin Martyr (**16.4**), Irenaeus (**16.5**), Clement of Alexandria (**16.6**), Tertullian (**16.7**), Theodotus (**16.8**) and Origen (**16.9**) occasionally preserve gems. Sayings have been discovered not only in the Koran (17.1–5) and in various Moslem writers (17.6–29), but also in unexpected places such as a ruined mosque in India (17.30) or rubbish heaps outside Egyptian villages (chapters 5 and 6). For over a century, priceless papyrus fragments (**5.1**) have been discovered. Sayings of Jesus hitherto unknown have been brought to the light of day.

7 Legitimacy of using the Apocrypha

In spite of the fact that authentic sayings may be uncovered in the Coptic *Gospel of Thomas* and elsewhere, it has to be stressed that none of the apocryphal gospels will ever be included within the canon of the New Testament. As we saw in chapter 1, the canon was closed once and for all in the fifth century; and rightly so. Much inferior matter has been incorporated into some of these other documents under the influence of extreme asceticism or other heretical views.

Is it therefore legitimate to use these gospels and other sources? I think it is. In all our study of Scripture, the most important matter is to discover the mind of Jesus behind the words recorded by different evangelists within the New Testament. Yet even one of their number admitted that he had had to be very selective in his choice of material for his gospel (John 21.25). If some sayings of Jesus have been recorded outside the canonical gospels, they also should be examined for possible clues. There may indeed be hidden treasure waiting to be uncovered. It may be that fresh light can be shed on the text of the New Testament and on the teaching of Jesus by the study of these extra-canonical documents and sayings. Even though most scholars ignore the existence of this material outside the New Testament, it has been claimed that one cannot properly understand what is included in the canon unless one understands what was excluded from it.[3]

The question of authenticity is one to which we turn in the next chapter.

CHAPTER THREE

Separating the Gold from the Dross

1 Testing for Authenticity

How can we judge whether or not particular sayings go back to Jesus? This question has to be asked not only of non-canonical sayings, but also of those recorded within the New Testament. If there is a different version in each of the three synoptic gospels (Matthew, Mark and Luke) and perhaps another version in John's Gospel, which is most likely to be closest to what Jesus actually said? Which are authentic and which are less likely to be so?

2 How to study the New Testament

Since the beginning of the twentieth century, New Testament scholars have used various methods in their attempts to discover the earliest form of the words of Jesus.

In the nineteenth and early twentieth centuries, scholars were concerned about questions of authorship and sources. Did Matthew, Mark, Luke and John write the four gospels attributed to them? What sources did the evangelists use? Were these sources oral or written? In 1924, B. H. Streeter published his book on the four gospels.[1] In this, he argued for four written documents lying behind Matthew and Luke. Mark was one of these four. The others were Q (standing for the German word *Quelle* meaning 'source') – the common source used by Matthew and Luke, M – special material used by Matthew, and L – special material used by Luke. Nowadays, it would be fairly widely recognized that there were at least two written documents.

Mark's Gospel as we find it in the New Testament was the earliest gospel and was used by Matthew and Luke. There may also have been another written source – the hypothetical document known as Q.[2] This has completely disappeared except for the passages in Matthew and Luke that are virtually identical in wording. The other two – M and L – may have been documents used respectively by Matthew and Luke or they may simply have been material passed on by word of mouth.[3]

3 Sermon Illustrations

Such literary and source criticism was supplemented immediately after the First World War by form criticism. Three German scholars led the way in this – K. L. Schmidt, Otto Dibelius and Rudolf Bultmann. This was an attempt to discover the original forms of the gospel material – pronouncement stories, miracle stories, sayings of Jesus, legends and myths. These various types of material originated in the early Church. They did not necessarily go back to Jesus. They may simply have been illustrations in sermons or stories used in Christian teaching. It was Dibelius who suggested preaching as the context within which some of the material within the gospels was originally preserved. Other sayings of Jesus could have been used, or even created, in the course of arguments with Jews over, for example, the observance of the sabbath (4.7; 6.2; 10.34) or the value of circumcision (10.20). As Graham Stanton has put it, 'Form critics emphasize that Jesus traditions were transmitted in order to sustain the life of the church rather than to provide bald reminiscence.'[4]

4 Editing the Material

Form criticism was followed after the Second World War by redaction criticism with studies by another three German scholars – Günther Bornkamm, Hans Conzelmann and Willi Marxsen. This recognizes that each of the evangelists was more than a collector of material, written or oral. Each one was an editor (redactor) and even a theologian in his own right. The theological standpoint of each evangelist is shown by the way in which he edited his source material.

5 How much can we know about Jesus?

Each of these methods can be used as part of the process of discovering the original words of Jesus and of assessing their authenticity. Yet one of the results of form criticism was to suggest that we can know little, if anything, about the historical Jesus. All that we can discover is how a particular passage of Scripture was used in the early Church. As far as Jesus himself is concerned, it was argued that all that matters is the fact that he was a historical figure. We cannot really know anything about what he said or did. This would mean that we cannot be sure of the authenticity of any of the sayings of Jesus, not even those in the canonical gospels. They may all have been put into his mouth by the early Church or by the writers of the gospels. What he actually said is hidden from us. What we hear from the gospels is only the whisper of the voice of Jesus.[5]

This extreme position produced extreme reactions in both directions. Some Protestant scholars rejected the authenticity of the traditions contained within the synoptic gospels (Matthew, Mark and Luke). They argued that we could not possibly know anything at all about the life and ministry of Jesus.

On the other hand, Joachim Jeremias and Roman Catholic scholars regarded the first three gospels as being substantially faithful to fact. Many other Protestant scholars, especially in Britain, have come to feel that we can know very much more about the work and words of Jesus than some form critics maintained.

It has now been almost universally agreed that the evangelists were not mere collectors and handers-on of traditional material. Redaction criticism has emphasized the fact that the evangelists were real authors with a theology of their own and not mere collectors of oral or written tradition. Yet even though the evangelists were theologians as well as editors, they do give us a faithful picture of the life and teaching of Jesus. The canonical gospels are, in the main, historically reliable as sources for the life and ministry of Jesus, even though they are not biographies in the modern sense of that term. Nor are they verbatim reports of the teaching of Jesus.[6]

6 Aramaic Words of Jesus

Some years ago, Protestant scholars like Matthew Black and Joachim Jeremias[7] attempted to recover some of the words of Jesus through a study of Aramaic. Although the New Testament was originally written in Hellenistic Greek, the mother tongue of Jesus was Aramaic, a language akin to Hebrew. He may well have been able to speak Greek, but it was probably in Aramaic, not in Greek, that he preached to the ordinary people of Palestine.

Most of the New Testament writers also spoke Aramaic as their mother tongue. In certain cases, it is possible that they wrote first drafts of their books in Aramaic or made use of Aramaic written sources. In particular, it is likely that the sayings source lying behind the Gospels of Matthew and Luke was an Aramaic document.[8]

Mark's Gospel, the first to be written, has retained the Aramaic words spoken by Jesus in his mother tongue on certain occasions. In the story of the raising of the daughter of Jairus, we find the words spoken by Jesus to the little girl, '*Talitha cum*' (Mark 5.41). These are the same words that her mother might have used when rousing her daughter in the morning. To a deaf and dumb man, Jesus said, '*Ephphatha*' (Mark 7.34 – 'be opened'). Mark tells us that, in his prayer in the Garden of Gethsemane, Jesus addressed God as '*Abba*' (Mark 14.36). Finally, Mark records Aramaic words spoken by Jesus on the cross, '*Eli, Eli, lama sabachthani?*' (Mark 15.34 – 'My God, my God, why have you forsaken me?') – a quotation from Psalm 22.1. In these four incidents recorded by Mark, we may have the actual words of Jesus.

7 Parables of Jesus

In our search for reliable clues to the content of the teaching of Jesus, we can consider his parables. It is difficult to find rabbinical parallels to these before the time of Jesus. There are a few examples in the Old Testament: for example, Nathan's parable of the poor man's ewe lamb (2 Samuel 12.1–7) and Isaiah's parable of the vineyard (Isaiah 5.1–7). The synoptic gospels (see **3.1**) give us fifty or sixty parables of Jesus. To these we must add about a dozen short parables in the Fourth Gospel, including the apprenticed son (John 5.19f.), the traveller at sunset (John 12.35), the woman in labour (John 16.21) and the Father's house (John 14.2). Such short passages have as much right to be regarded as authentic parables as the longer stories in the synoptic gospels though even in those three gospels there are also short parables.[9]

In all these parables, we are in close touch with the teaching of Jesus. Here we have reliable tradition about his method and message, especially if we can go behind the Greek text to the underlying Aramaic tradition. By studying the versions of parables in each of the three synoptic gospels (as well as those in the Coptic *Gospel of Thomas* – see chapter 9), we can try to discover what Jesus said and how he said it. This is the value of having two or three accounts which look at the same incident or story from different points of view – giving a synopsis or viewing together (*sun* – together; *opsis* – viewing).

8 Sayings of Jesus in the Fourth Gospel

In the past, it was argued that the many differences between the Fourth Gospel and the other three cast doubt upon its historical reliability. Yet it is possible that the fourth evangelist wrote independently of Matthew, Mark and Luke. He may have drawn subject matter from his own oral or written sources. This may take us back as early as, if not earlier than, they do. John may even have had an Aramaic sayings source similar to that used by Matthew and Luke.[10]

While the long discourses in John's Gospel may have been composed by the evangelist, hidden within them there may be genuine sayings of Jesus. Not only so; but this gospel encourages us to look for authentic words outside the New Testament. We are reminded that Jesus did many other signs 'not recorded in this book' (John 20.30) and that 'there are many other things that Jesus did, which, if written in detail, the world would not hold the books that would be written' (John 21.25). We can therefore expect to find hidden treasure outside the four gospels.

9 Nag Hammadi Library

Some of those places where hidden treasure may be discovered are apocryphal gospels, including those found at Chenoboskion near the River Nile (7.1–7). From the time of the discovery of this remarkable library in 1945 till about 1978, it was almost universally held by scholars that what had been accidentally brought back to the light of day was the remains of a gnostic library. Up to recent years, gnosticism has been known mainly from attacks made upon it by orthodox Christians. When these old books were discovered, it was presumed that most, if not all, of the documents contained within them were gnostic in origin. They could, therefore, be of little historical value apart from what light they might shed on the history and thought of this second-century heresy. They contained not what Jesus actually said, but what heretics wished he had said. So it was argued.[11]

On the other hand, if one starts off with an examination of the documents themselves, one can come up with other conclusions. Some of these writings may have been written by heretics, but one must not start off with the assumption that all of them had such a beginning. They are not all of the same kind. Some of the books are pagan, some apocryphal but not necessarily heretical. One should not presume that only sayings that can be paralleled in the canonical gospels have any chance of being authentic words of Jesus.

10 *Gospel of Thomas*

The most interesting and exciting of all the documents in the Nag Hammadi Library is the Coptic *Gospel of Thomas*. Just as John's Gospel goes back to Aramaic oral tradition independently of the synoptic gospels, so *Thomas* may go back to an early and independent Syriac tradition. Buried beneath the rubble of extreme asceticism or encratism (8.14), new and genuine sayings of Jesus otherwise unknown may lie hidden. Where parallels to the canonical gospels exist, these may shed fresh light on the meaning of sayings of Jesus in the New Testament. As the Jesus Seminar (see note 6) has admitted: 'The *Gospel of Thomas* has proved to be a gold mine of comparative material and new information.'[12]

Five sayings in *Thomas* are virtually identical with words spoken by Jesus in the canonical gospels (9.20; 10.14; 12.16, 19, 26). In addition, another seventy-three sayings contain parallels to, or echoes of, words of Jesus in the New Testament. These also may include authentic tradition.

Thomas contains fifteen parables (**8.4; 9.2**), of which twelve are independent versions of parables in the synoptic gospels. It is possible that in certain cases we may be nearer to the parable as originally taught by Jesus.

It is even possible that some of the sayings in *Thomas* without canonical parallels or echoes, including the three non-canonical parables, may preserve teaching given by Jesus during his ministry in Palestine. Each saying must be examined carefully on its own merits and compared with other material, both Christian and gnostic, in order to determine its authenticity.

11 Tests of Authenticity

How, then, are we to decide which sayings are authentic and which are not? How can we become skilled money-changers, rejecting some but retaining the good (16.12, 22, 23)?

In addition to the various methods of New Testament study already discussed, certain tests of authenticity have been proposed. While there is no universally agreed list of criteria, there are some which can be applied in our study of the sayings hidden in apocryphal documents and elsewhere as in the study of the New Testament. They fall into two main categories: external evidence and internal.

By external evidence is meant the source or sources from which the sayings are quoted. If these are early and reliable, and especially if there are several of them and they are independent of each other, then the saying can be regarded as being authentic.

Internal evidence refers to the content of the saying itself. Does it match up to what we already know of the mind of Jesus from other sources, in particular the gospels within the canon of the New Testament? Is it similar to his teaching already familiar to us? Is it different from that of Judaism?[13]

12 Multiple Attestation

One of the most common tests is that of multiple attestation. If a saying has been preserved in two or more gospel sources that are independent of each other (Mark, Q, M, L), it is probably a genuine saying of Jesus. This is especially true if it is also attested elsewhere, for example, in one of Paul's letters.

If one accepts the independence of *Thomas* and its early date, then this sayings document can be added as another witness in addition to the four gospel sources. If a saying occurs in either Mark or Q or M or L and also in *Thomas*, it may go back to Jesus.[14]

For example, Jesus' prohibition of divorce is found not only in Mark 10.2–12 and reproduced in Matthew 19.3–12. It is also recorded in a passage from Q as seen in Matthew 5.31f. and Luke 16.18. Moreover, quite independently of the gospels, Paul refers to a dominical saying in 1 Corinthians 7.10f.

Similarly, there are several versions of the words of institution of the Lord's Supper. The oldest is that in 1 Corinthians 11.23–25. This is the one still used at present-day communion services. Mark 14.22–24 has a slightly different version expanded in Matthew 26.26–28. Luke 22.17–20 has another independent narrative. Despite all the minor variations, the essential elements in the narrative are the same. Paul has recorded the command to repeat the celebration in connection with the handing over of the cup (4.3). This is also found in a fourth-century document, the *Apostolic Constitutions*, which also has the interesting idea of putting extra words into the mouth of Jesus (16.34).

Examples of sayings in *Thomas* also found in one or more gospel sources are those about a blind man leading a blind man (Q and *Thomas* 34 – 10.14); a rejected prophet (Mark and *Thomas* 31 – 11.6); holes for foxes and nests for birds (Q and *Thomas* 86 – 11.8).

13 Explanation of Grading

In the following chapters, sayings attributed to Jesus will be translated into English and given a grading to indicate possible authenticity. In the case of sayings recorded only outside the New Testament, the test of multiple attestation may be more difficult to apply. There is no real problem with regard to those that are virtually identical with the canonical text, especially with Mark or Q. In the grading from A to D, these will normally be marked with an A. Where a saying is very close to one or more in the New Testament, it is quite possibly authentic and will be marked with a B. Where it is obviously true to the spirit of Jesus as we know that from our reading of the New Testament but there is no clear canonical parallel, it will be given a C rating. Sayings which are of doubtful authenticity will be marked with a D.

It must be clearly recognized that such grading is subjective and personal. It is to be regarded only as a guide to possible authenticity and may be regarded by some as being arbitrary. Other people may differ in their evaluation of particular sayings.

14 Traces of Aramaic

Another test of authenticity that will be used has already been mentioned – that of traces of Aramaic. At least one scholar dismissed this criterion as being a dubious one on the ground that others besides Jesus spoke Aramaic. However, here it will be used not so much as a test of authenticity as a way of reaching the original message through the understanding of possible mistranslations from Aramaic into Greek on the part of the evangelists (9.2).

Provided the apocryphal sayings are used with caution and without undue dogmatism, fresh light may be shed by at least some of them on the text of the New Testament and on the meaning of the message of Jesus.

Part Two

Early Gold Mines

CHAPTER FOUR

Words of the Lord

1 Apostolic Authority

With this chapter, we come to the real purpose of this book – the study of actual or alleged sayings of Jesus. All that has gone before has been by way of introduction, attempting to place them in their context either inside or outside the New Testament and to suggest methods of deciding whether or not they are genuine.

As we have already noted (1.4), one of the motives at work in the choice of books for the New Testament was the great authority attached by Christians to sayings that could be traced back to Jesus through the apostles. There are several references to such words of the Lord in the New Testament itself outside the four gospels. So we shall start by uncovering the most likely of these since they are, strictly speaking, within the canon. Thereafter, we shall consider some sayings not found in modern versions of the Bible since they are not recorded in the earliest manuscripts. In order to understand the situation more clearly, we require to consider briefly some of the Greek texts available to New Testament scholars.

2 Manuscripts

The original documents may have been written on rolls of papyrus (5.1) but all of them have perished. Many fragments of papyrus, some containing a few verses, some only a few words or lines, have survived but none of them go back earlier than the second century. Most scholars believe that the earliest known fragment, referred to as p^{52} and containing part of John 18.31–34, 37, 38, can be dated to about AD 125. Since this has writing on both sides, it must have been in the form of a book rather than in the form of a roll.

The book form was known as a codex. Sheets of papyrus and later of parchment were bound together like a modern book. This made it possible for scribes to write on both sides of the leaf or page. Not only so, it was easier to turn to a particular passage in a codex. The two earliest and best complete copies of the New Testament date from about the middle of the fourth century AD and are known as Codex Sinaiticus (discovered in the monastery of St Catherine on Mount Sinai in the middle of the nineteenth century) and Codex Vaticanus (which has been in the Vatican library since before 1475). Neither of these two great manuscripts was available to scholars when the Authorized Version was published in 1611. This was translated from what came to be known as the 'received text', which was based on a Greek text compiled from a few inferior manuscripts by Erasmus and printed in 1516.

Those who wish to pursue the fascinating story of textual criticism can do so with the aid of various books.[1] For the purpose of our present study, two later codices are important since they contain extra sayings of Jesus.

Codex Bezae is a sixth-century manuscript well-known for additions to the Greek text. It was presented to Cambridge University Library by the Reformer, Theodore Bezae, in 1581. It is also interesting on account of the fact that it has Greek on the left-hand page and Latin on the right.

Codex 700 dates from the eleventh century.

3 Outside the Four Gospels

4.1 – Acts 11.16   c

John baptized with water, but you will be baptized in Holy Spirit.

In his report to the church at Jerusalem, Peter declared how, when Gentiles received the Holy Spirit, he remembered this prediction of the Lord. It is also quoted in Acts 1.5 with the addition of the phrase, 'after these few days'. In Mark 1.8, it is John the Baptist himself who made this contrast between his own baptism of people and that of Jesus. It has been suggested that the saying has been transferred by Luke from the lips of John to the lips of Jesus, making Peter's speech end with a saying of Jesus like the speech of Paul in Act 20.35 (4.2).

4.2 – Acts 20.35 B

It is more blessed to keep on giving than to keep on receiving.

In his farewell speech to the Ephesian elders, Paul recalls these words of the Lord Jesus. They encourage the constant and continuous attitude of mind that wishes to keep on giving rather than to be receiving from others.[2] The kind of life that seeks to give and to serve rather than to get earns a reward both here and hereafter. Happiness consists in constant giving rather than in constantly being a recipient. Yet discernment in giving is added in Ephesians 4.28, where giving to those in need is recommended. What is being extolled in Acts 20.35 is not the isolated charitable act, but the constant and continuous attitude of mind that wishes to keep on giving. Such also is the grace of God, the divine love that takes the initiative in giving to human beings. This was seen especially in the life and ministry of Jesus. J. H. Ropes considered this to be a genuine saying of Jesus, but others are not so sure. Ernst Haenchen, for example, believes that Luke has taken up a Greek proverb and placed it in the mouth of Jesus, as in Acts 26.14: 'It is hard for you to kick against the goads.'[3]

4.3 – 1 Corinthians 11.25 A

Keep on doing this as often as you drink that God may remember me.

Only in Luke 22.19 and in 1 Corinthians 11.24 is the command given to repeat the act of breaking and eating bread. Luke omits the command given here by Paul with regard to the cup. Usually, the last phrase is translated into English as, 'in remembrance of me'; but this obscures a possible meaning of the words of Jesus, which can be translated literally as, 'into my remembrance'. Jesus may have intended the sacrament to be a reminder to God of the sacrifice of Jesus as the inauguration of the new covenant – an intercessory prayer that, in spite of our human failings, God will remain faithful to his side of the covenant and bring about his good purpose for human beings, the coming of his kingdom in all its fullness.[4]

4.4 – 1 Thessalonians 4.15 c

For this we say to you in a word of the Lord,
that we who are left alive
until the coming of the Lord
will not precede those who fall asleep.

Paul seems to be quoting here a word of the Lord, at least indirectly. The problem is where this saying ends. Does it take in the following verses as well, and if so, how many of them? It has been argued that these words were simply Paul's introductory summary of the actual saying which follows in verses 16 and 17a, again in indirect speech:

For the Lord himself on a word of command,
at the sound of an archangel and a trumpet-call,
will descend from heaven
and the dead in Christ will rise first,
then we who are left alive
shall be caught up with them in the clouds
to meet the Lord in the air.

Then Paul adds his own words of comfort in 17b and 18:

And so we shall be
for ever with the Lord.
Therefore comfort one another with these words.

Whichever verses comprise the saying, we cannot have it in its
exact form since Jesus would not have referred to himself as 'the
Lord' nor would he have spoken in the first person plural, 'we
who are left alive' (verses 15 and 17). In spite of the problems,
Joachim Jeremias regarded verses 16 and 17a (not verse 15) as
'the oldest of the sayings outside the gospels' and declares that
'there is no reason why this should not be a genuine saying of
Jesus'.[5] I myself am not so sure. Various possibilities have been
suggested. Paul may be summarizing what he regards as the
essential teaching of Jesus about his second coming, or he may be
quoting the words of the exalted Jesus given through a prophet
or even through himself, or the saying may be drawn from some
Jewish or early Christian apocalyptic writing now lost.[6]

4 From Gospel Manuscripts

4.5 – Matthew 20.28 (Codex Bezae)   B

**Seek to increase from little
and not from greater to be less**

This follows Jesus' teaching that, unlike great men of the world,
disciples should become great by serving, following his own
example. They should, on the one hand, think highly of their
lowly service for the gospel, as Paul did (Romans 11.13), but at
the same time should not think too highly of themselves,
considering others to be better than themselves (Philippians 2.3).
This is illustrated with advice about what to do when invited to
dinner which appears to have been based on Luke 14.8–14 – the
parable about guests taking their places at a marriage feast. 'Don't
take the highest places,' Jesus says in effect, 'in case someone
more important comes later and you are asked by your host to
give your seat to that person and take a lower place yourself.'

4.6 – Mark 9.49 (Codex Bezae)   D

Every sacrifice will be salted with salt.

The scribe who was copying the manuscript seems to have been reminded of this rule from Leviticus 2.13 by the verb in the previous saying, 'For everyone will be salted with fire.'

4.7 – Luke 6.5 (Codex Bezae)   A

Fellow, happy are you
if you know what you are doing;
but if you do not know,
you are accursed and a transgressor of the law.

This comes in a short story in place of Luke 6.5, which is transferred to follow verse 10. While it is not part of the original text of Luke's Gospel, it could be a genuine saying.[7] Jesus has found someone working on the sabbath. These words, at first sight, seem to countenance the breaking of the sabbath law. Yet they are really a warning against thoughtless transgression. Only if one knows that Jesus is greater than anything or anyone else is it permissible to dispense with this rule. So this is a graphic illustration of the truth of the saying that it displaces about Jesus being Lord even of the sabbath.

4.8 – Luke 9.55 (Codex Bezae)   B

You do not know of what manner of spirit you are;
for the Son of man did not come
to destroy people's lives
but to save them.

In this case, only the first line occurs in Codex Bezae. The rest of the saying is found in other late manuscripts. It is possible that these words were used in Jesus' rebuke to the disciples. They are translated in the Authorized Version but relegated to footnotes in modern English versions. A scribe may have inserted them in the margin with Luke 19.10 in mind:

For the Son of man came
to seek and to save the lost.

Compare a similar insertion at Matthew 18.11, also in Codex
Bezae, without the first line of the saying in Luke 9.55:

> *For the Son of man came*
> *to save the lost.*

4.9 – Luke 11.2 (Codex 700)   D

Let your Holy Spirit come upon us and purify us.

Although this variant reading is not found in any manuscript
before this eleventh-century codex, it is possible that Marcion
(second century) knew a version of the Lord's Prayer that
contained this reference to the Holy Spirit. Gregory of Nyssa
(fourth century) also testified to this reading in one of the
gospels. Perhaps it originated as a scribe's explanation in the
margin of the phrase, 'Your kingdom come.' B. H. Streeter, on
the other hand, maintained that this is probably what Luke
wrote.[8]

4.10 – John 5.7, 10, 11 (Codex Bezae)   A

> *Let one of you who is without sin*
> *be first to throw a stone at her.*
> *Woman, where are they?*
> *Did no one condemn you?*
> *Neither do I condemn you;*
> *go, from now on do not sin.*

This is such a familiar story to those of us brought up on the
Authorized Version that it may come as a surprise to learn that it
is not found in any of the early manuscripts of the New
Testament. It occurs in Codex Bezae and other late authorities.
It could nevertheless be genuine. It shows the attitude of Jesus
towards sinners that is characteristic especially of Luke's Gospel.
Moreover, it has been suggested that, by stooping down and
writing with his finger in the dust, Jesus was imitating the action
of a Roman judge.[9] Before passing sentence he wrote it down on

a tablet and then read it aloud. So when Jesus was pressed to give a reply, he read out to the woman's accusers what he had written in the dust:

> ***Let one of you who is without sin***
> ***be first to throw a stone at her.***

CHAPTER FIVE

Scraps of Old Paper

1 What is Papyrus?

Papyrus (4.2) is the ancient writing material from which the English word 'paper' is derived. It was made from reeds or bulrushes that grow in marshy spots like the Nile Delta, as was also the basket made for the baby Moses by his mother (Exodus 2.3).

From the eighteenth century onwards, countless fragments of papyrus have been recovered from rubbish dumps in Egypt. These scraps are the remains of documents of various kinds written between the first century BC and the seventh century AD. Some are less preserved than others and consist mainly of fresh air. They include fragments of Greek and Latin literary texts, known and unknown.

2 Egerton Papyrus 2

Most important of all are the Christian texts, one of which is known as Egerton Papyrus 2 from the name of the fund used to purchase it for the British Museum, where it now resides.[1] It contains words from an unknown gospel. Since it has been dated to around AD 150, it is one of the oldest pieces of Christian writing to survive the centuries. It comprises two leaves plus fragments of a third and contains the remains of four short passages. Gaps in manuscripts are indicated by ellipses (. . .) while square brackets are used to give suggested restorations of the text.

3 First Passage

5.1 c

[Punish ev]ery lawbreaker and lawless person
and not me; for . . .

The text of this first saying otherwise unknown is so fragmentary
that one can only guess how it began and how it ended. Jesus
said something to the lawyers about punishing or convicting
lawbreakers rather than himself.

5.2 A

Those scriptures which you search
(and) in which you think you have life
are the ones which bear witness concerning me.

From the lawyers, Jesus turned to the rulers of the people with
words similar to John 5.39:

You search the scriptures
because you think that in them you have eternal life;
and it is they that bear witness concerning me.

The slight difference in wording is exactly the shade of meaning
found in some Latin and Syriac manuscripts.

5.3 A

Do not think that I came to accuse you to my Father.
There is one who accuses, Moses,
in whom you have set your hope.

This saying repeats almost word for word John 5.45.

5.4 c

Now your unbelief is being accused.

This was the final conclusion to the incident. The audience kept on repeating words similar to those addressed by the Pharisees to the man born blind in John 9.29. They knew that God spoke to Moses but did not know from where Jesus came, in spite of the fact that Moses had written about Jesus (John 5.46).

---

4 Second Passage

5.5 A

I do wish! Be cleansed!
Go and show yourself to the priests.

On the other side of the first fragment, there is the conclusion of a story in which Jesus escapes from the clutches of his enemies, as in John 7.30. It is followed by an account of the healing of a leper, very similar to that found in Matthew 8.2–4; Mark 1.40–44; Luke 5.12–14. An interesting extra detail is that the leper describes how he became a leper by travelling and eating with lepers. This may have been an attempt to enlist the sympathy of Jesus. It was while he was going about his daily life that he contracted this loathsome disease.

---

5 Third passage

5.6 A

Why do you call me Teacher
while you do not listen to what I say?
It was of you that Isaiah so rightly prophesied
when he said,
'Th[is people] honours me only with lip-service
but their [hear]t is [far from] me.
In vain they [worship me]
. . . commandments.'

Jesus has been asked, not about paying tax to Caesar as in

Matthew 22.17; Mark 12.14; Luke 20.22; *Thomas*100 (12.29), but more generally about what it is appropriate to give to the ruling power. In Luke 6.46, the accusation of not doing what Jesus says is given a different setting, as the introduction to the parable of the two houses. In Matthew 15.7–9 and Mark 7.6f., the quotation from Isaiah 29.13 is cited within the context of a denunciation of the Pharisees and scribes for their use of the tradition of the elders concerning ritual washing to break the written law of God. It is possible that, in the original form of the discussion between Jesus and his questioners, these words were used as an introduction to his rejoinder about giving Caesar Caesar's and God God's. This ending has been lost in Egerton Papyrus 2 on account of the mutilation of the papyrus fragment.[2]

---

6 Fourth Passage

5.7 c

[When a farmer has locked up]
[a small seed in a hid]den place
[so that] it has been invisibly buried
[how] does its abundance be[come] immeasurable?

The fourth passage describes a miracle performed by Jesus. it begins with this tantalizingly fragmented question translated from the tentative restoration suggested by C. H. Dodd.[3] When the people were perplexed by this strange rhetorical question, Jesus scattered a handful of seeds on the river bank and they immediately brought forth fruit.

CHAPTER SIX

From Egyptian
Rubbish Heaps

1 Oxyrhynchus

In addition to Egerton Papyrus 2, there are thousands of papyrus fragments from various sites in Egypt. Some were discovered in tombs – some even stuffed inside mummified crocodiles, considered to be divine by ancient Egyptians. The vast majority came from rubbish dumps on the outskirts of ancient villages and towns. One of these was Oxyrhynchus, a village about 200 miles north of Nag Hammadi and ten miles west of the River Nile. While many of these fragments contain pieces of New Testament text, there are a few that preserve sayings of Jesus not recorded in the four gospels.[1]

Three of the Oxyrhynchus Papyri (1, 654 and 655) appear to be fragments of a Greek edition of the *Gospel of Thomas*, a Coptic version of which was discovered at Chenoboskion in 1945 (**7.1**). This may have been the complete text of the document that was later translated into Coptic. It is more likely that both go back independently to an apocryphal gospel or collection of sayings of Jesus attributed to *Thomas*.

Sayings that are paralleled in the Coptic version will be briefly discussed in this chapter. Further comments will be reserved until we come to deal with *Thomas* in chapters 10 to 12.

2 Oxyrhynchus Papyrus 1

This leaf of papyrus was discovered in 1897 and contains several sayings which also occur in the Coptic *Gospel of Thomas* 26 to

41

33, 77 (12.13; 10.34; 11.9; 10.10; 11.16; 11.6; 12.14; 15; 11.17, respectively).

6.1 A

. . . and then you will see clearly
to take out the speck
in your brother's eye.

This is almost word for word the ending of the saying in Matthew 7.5 and Luke 6.42 (Q). The whole saying occurs in *Thomas* 26 (12.13).

6.2 C

If you do not fast from the world,
you will not find the kingdom of God,
and if you do not keep the sabbath as sabbath
you will not see the Father.

The Coptic form of this saying is found in *Thomas* 27 (10.34).

6.3 D

I stood in the midst of the world
and in human form I appeared to them
and found them all drunk
and no one among them thirsty
and my soul is troubled for the sons of men,
because they are blind in their heart
and do not see . . .

There is a longer conclusion to this saying in *Thomas* 28 (11.9). A lamentation on the lips of Jesus over the blindness of people, it looks like a mixture of phrases from the New Testament, such as John 1.14, John 7.37, 1 Thessalonians 5.7, 1 John 4.2, 2 John 7, and from Isaiah 53.11.

6.4 D

. . . *poverty.*

Only one Greek word survives of this saying, but the full Coptic
text is preserved in *Thomas* 29 (10.10).

6.5 A

**Wherever there are [two] [they are not] without God
and where one is alone I say I am with him.
Raise the stone and you will find me there;
split the wood and I am there.**

This is one of the most famous of all the sayings of Jesus outside
the New Testament. In the Coptic version, it is found in two
parts – *Thomas* 30 (11.16) and *Thomas* 77 (11.17). The first part
looks like an expanded version of the saying of Jesus found in
Matthew 18.20. The promise, however, is not simply of the
divine fellowship whenever two or three Christians meet, but of
the realization of the presence of the living Jesus by a single
disciple. In *Thomas* 77 (11.17) the two parts of the second half of
this fragment are found in reverse order.

6.6 A

**A prophet is not acceptable in his own country
neither does a doctor work cures on those who know him.**

This is an expansion, found also in *Thomas* 31 (11.6), of Luke
4.24 and John 4.44.

6.7 A

**A city built on a high mountain
and fortified
cannot fall or be hidden.**

There can be little doubt concerning the authenticity of this saying in one form or another, since it is found in at least two independent sources. The slight variations from Matthew 5.14 ('high mountain', 'fortified' and 'cannot fall') recur in *Thomas* 32 (12.14).

6.8 D

You hear with your one ear
[but the other ear you have closed].

The words in square brackets are one suggestion for the restoration of this saying. If this is correct, Jesus is complaining that his message has been imperfectly heard and understood. However, this does not fit in with the complete version in *Thomas* 33 (12.15), which gives a different conclusion.

---

3 Oxyrhynchus Papyrus 654

Oxyrynchus Papyrus 654 was discovered in 1903. Originally a document concerned with property, the back of this papyrus was later used by someone to copy out – at the end of the second century or the beginning of the third century AD – certain sayings of Jesus from an earlier original. These sayings in Greek are similar to those in *Thomas* 1 to 7 (10.1, 2, 24, 27, 32, 17; 9.16).

6.9 C

These are the words which . . .
the living Jesus spoke
. . . (who is) also (called) Thomas and spoke . . .
'. . . these words . . . he will not taste . . .'

The Coptic version of this Greek fragment appears in the Preface and first saying in *Thomas* (10.1).

6.10 C

Let not him who is se[eking] . . . has found
and when he has found . . . has wondered
he will reign and . . . find rest.

To the asking, seeking and finding of Matthew 7.7 have been added not only wondering and reigning, found also in *Thomas* 2 (10.2), but also finding rest, an idea found in Matthew 11.28 and in the *Gospel of the Hebrews*, according to Clement of Alexandria (15.11 and 12).

6.11 B

. . . who lead us . . . the kingdom in hea[ven] . . .
the birds of hea[ven] . . .
what is under the earth . . .
the fish of the se[a]
. . . you. And the kingdom . . . is within you . . .
he who knows will fi[nd this] . . .
you will know yourselves . . .
you are of the Father, of the . . .
you know yourselves in . . . and you are poverty.

The gaps in the Greek text can be tentatively filled out by reference to the Coptic text in *Thomas* 3 (10.24). In the parallel saying in Luke 17.21, the kingdom of God is said to be 'amongst you' or 'in the midst of you' while here, as in *Thomas* 3, the meaning is clearly 'within you'. It is equated with the self-knowledge of those who know they are children of their heavenly Father. Such are 'the poor in spirit' who are truly happy (Matthew 5.3).

6.12 D

A m[an] will not hesitate . . . to ask a [child] . . .
about the place of the . . .

> **Then many (first) will [be the last and]**
> **the last the first and . . .**

The meaning of this fragment has been clarified through comparison with *Thomas* 4 (10.27).

6.13   c

> **. . . lies (before) your eye and . . .**
> **from you will be uncovered . . .**
> **[nothing] is hidden that will not be revealed,**
> **and buried that will not be raised up.**

The last line is an addition to the saying as found in *Thomas* 5 (10.32). It has been suggested that the reason for this omission is that the idea of resurrection is incompatible with gnostic teaching, but that is to presume that *Thomas* is a gnostic document. The phrase is also missing from the synoptic versions (see comment on 10.32).

6.14   c

> **. . . do not . . .**
> **. . . truth . . .**
> **. . . hidden . . .**

The papyrus becomes more and more fragmentary as it proceeds. Its wording and meaning can be guessed at from *Thomas* 6 (10.17).

6.15   d

> **. . . happy . . .**

Of the final saying on this papyrus, only one Greek word can be deciphered. The rest must be completed from *Thomas* 7 (9.16).

---

4 Oxyrhynchus Papyrus 655

Amongst various fragments from a second- or third-century papyrus roll, edited in 1904 by Grenfell and Hunt, two or three pieces have been collected as a result of the discovery of various sayings found together in *Thomas* 36 to 39 (12.17, 7; 10.15).

6.16 B

From early until [late]
. . . from evenin[g unti]l early
[about food] for you, what you
should eat [or] about c[lothing]
[for you] what you should [put on]
much [bet]ter [are] you than [the lilies]
which card not nor spin.
If you have a [garment] . . . also.

6.17 C

Who can add to your age?
He himself will give to you your clothing.
When you undress and are not ashamed . . .

6.18 C

. . . they have [obtained the keys]
of the [kingdom and] have hidden them.
[They themselves] go [not] in [and those]
who [wish to go] in [they have]
not al[lowed to go in. But you]
be wise as [serpents and without] guile [as do]ves.

---

5 Oxyrhynchus Papyrus 840

In 1905, a small, worm-eaten parchment leaf with writing on

both sides was discovered at Oxyrhynchus. It may be part of a tiny gospel book bought by an Egyptian woman for her child to wear round the neck as a protection from evil spirits. It contains forty-five lines of Greek words giving an otherwise unknown saying of Jesus and a story about his encounter with a Pharisee in the Temple.

6.19 c

First, before doing wrong
he reasons it all out subtly.
But be on your guard lest even you suffer
the same things as they do;
for not only among the living
do evil-doers among men receive punishment
but also they await retribution and much torment.

The first seven lines contain the conclusion of a discourse spoken by Jesus on the way to the Temple. The cunning preparation of a criminal for his crime is similar to that of the assassin in *Thomas* 98 (9.13). Here it is followed not only by punishment on earth but also by far worse torment hereafter. Jesus warns his disciples to be on their guard lest they also suffer a like fate.

6.20 c

And [immediately the Saviour stoo]d
w[ith his] disciples [and answered]:
'You also are here in the Temple court.
Are you clean?'
He said to him: 'I am clean;
for I washed in the pool of David
and went down by one stair
and came up by the other
and put on white and clean clothes
and only then did I come here

to look at these holy vessels.'
The Saviour said to him:
'Woe to you blind who do not see.
You washed in these waters poured out
in which dogs and pigs have lain night and day
and you washed yourself
and you chafed your outer skin,
which prostitutes [als]o and flute-girls anoint,
bathe, chafe and rouge,
in order to arouse desire in men,
but within they are full of scorpions
and of bad[ness of every kind].
But I and [my disciples] of whom you say
that we did not im[merse ourselves],
[have been immer]sed in the living [and pure] water
which comes down from [the Father in heaven].
[. . . B]ut woe to [t]hem . . .'

The warning to his disciples in the first seven lines (6.19) is
followed by the story of an encounter with a Pharisaic chief
priest named Levi, who remonstrated with Jesus for entering the
Temple and viewing the holy vessels without having bathed. His
disciples had not even washed their feet.

When first published in 1907, this was dismissed as a fantastic
invention on the ground that it showed ignorance of Jewish
custom at the time of Jesus. However, none of the objections are
valid. The forecourts of the Temple were surrounded by rooms in
which the Temple treasures were stored. John 11.55 and John
13.10 presuppose the need for ritual cleansing and the rule about
the washing only of feet thereafter. The contrast between outer
cleanliness and inner impurity is seen in such a passage as
Matthew 23.25; see *Thomas* 89 (10.21). Moreover, there is a
rabbinic parallel about a priest who boasted that he had entered
the temple precincts without washing his hands and feet. He was
asked how he had managed to escape the notice of the overseer.
So here, Jesus and his disciples were caught red-handed. Jesus
defended his apparent lack of respect for the Temple by

declaring that inner purity was more important than external cleanliness. Like the rule about washing one's hands before eating (Mark 7.3), such outward acts belonged to the tradition of the elders and not to God's law.[2]

---

6 Oxyrhynchus Papyrus 1224

This papyrus fragment has been dated by its writing to the beginning of the fourth century.

6.21 A

Pray for your enemies;
for he who is not [against yo]u is for you
[he who] is far off [today]
tomorrow will [b]ecome [near you].

The first two lines are reminiscent of Matthew 5.44 and Luke 9.50 respectively, while the antithesis of far and near also occurs in *Thomas* 82 (12.33), a saying quoted by Origen (16.20).

CHAPTER SEVEN

A Load of Old Books

1 Chenoboskion

One day in December 1945, Abu al-Majd and his oldest brother, Mohammed, discovered hidden treasure without realizing the tremendous implications of their find. Along with five other camel drivers, these Egyptian peasants were digging for fertilizer for their crops among chalky cliffs some two or three miles from the site of the ancient monastery of Chenoboskion, now known as El-Qasr.[1] In an abandoned cemetery, Abu unearthed a sealed four-handled red jar some twenty-four inches high and twelve inches wide at its broadest. Mohammed as eldest son took control. At first, he was afraid there might be an evil spirit inside; but then he thought it might contain treasure. So he took his mattock, shattered the jar and found twelve bound volumes and one loose pamphlet. He carefully wrapped them all in his tunic, threw the bundle over his shoulder, mounted his camel and carried home this load of old books. The two brothers did not appreciate the value of their find; for they allowed their mother to tear up and burn a few sheets in the kitchen stove. The rest were sold in Nag Hammadi for three Egyptian pounds to the son of a Coptic priest.

2 Nag Hammadi

Nag Hammadi is on the south bank of the River Nile and is the site of a barrage opened in 1930 to regulate the flood water and ensure irrigation of the neighbouring province. The documents sold in Nag Hammadi market came to be known as the Nag

Hammadi Library even though they were discovered near Chenoboskion on the opposite side of the river. One of them found its way by a roundabout route to Zurich, where it was deposited in the Jung Institute in 1952 and came to be known as the Jung Codex. It was eventually returned to Cairo – the last pages in 1975, after scholarly work on them was completed. The remaining volumes had previously been transferred to the Coptic Museum in Cairo but for many years were inaccessible for study and research. It was not until 1977 – thirty-two years after its discovery – that the complete library became available in a modern English translation.[2]

Altogether, these codices contain about fifty separate documents including a bad translation of Plato's *Republic* and other non-gnostic works. The second codex is the finest volume in the whole remarkable collection. It contains seven works, the second of which is the self-styled 'Gospel according to Thomas'.

3 Pachomian Monasteries

When the Nag Hammadi Library was first discovered in 1945, it was thought that it was the remains of a gnostic library that had, for some reason, been hidden away by a group of heretics living somewhere in the area. Nowadays, it is fairly widely held that it originated in a monastery or monasteries in the Thebaid.

These monasteries were founded by Pachomius, who was born in Upper Egypt of pagan parents about AD 290. When he was twenty years old, he was forcibly conscripted into the Roman army of Licinius, who ruled the Roman Empire side by side with Constantine for ten years. Some people brought food for the raw recruits who were being held in prison in an Egyptian town. 'Why are these people so good to us when they do not know us?' he asked his companions. They replied: 'They are Christians and they treat us with love for the sake of the God of heaven.' So Pachomius found the hidden treasure of the gospel because of the kindness of some unknown Christians. On being discharged from the army, he professed his faith and was baptized as a Christian in AD 313.[3]

Not only so; but Pachomius decided to go the second mile. He made up his mind to live an ascetic life as a hermit. There were many such hermits living in isolated caves and out-of-the-way spots near the River Nile. He joined another hermit, the aged Palaemon, whom he came to regard as his teacher and guide.

Pachomius, however, felt called to community life. He believed that God meant people to live together in social relationships. So he became the founder of what is known as coenobitic (common life) monasticism.[4] The first monastery he founded was at Tabennisi in the Thebaid, some 350 miles south of Cairo and about 150 miles north of Aswan and some sixty miles north of Luxor. Having moved there about AD 320, Pachomius had a dream in which he was told to build a monastery. This he did. There he gathered his first community, which he organized along quasi-military lines.

The second monastery to be founded was at Phbow and the third was at Chenoboskion, a Greek word meaning 'goose pasture'. This was a misnomer since, according to a first-century author, there was no grassland there for geese; but the inhabitants had a great veneration for crocodiles, of which there were many. The Coptic name of Chenoboskion was Sheneset, 'the acacias of Seth'. A chronicler of the fourth century wrote that it was 'a desert village, grilling in the intense heat. There were not many inhabitants, only a few.'[5]

By the time Pachomius died in AD 346, he had founded nine monasteries for men and two nunneries for women. These communities had some 5,000 members. He was succeeded by Petronius, who died shortly afterwards, and then by Theodore.

A few years earlier, some philosophers came from the town of Akhmim to bait Pachomius about the interpretation of Scripture. Pachomius sent out to them Theodore and two other monks. Theodore gave them a piece of his mind and cleverly turned the tables on them in the course of conversation. The philosophers said to him: 'You pride yourselves on knowing the scriptures as well as their interpretation. So now, tell us who was not born and died, who was born but did not die, who died but did not decay.' Theodore answered: 'Oh you whose mind is like a leaking barrel, dwindles like a breath and fades away! He who died not having been born was Adam; he who was born but did not die was Enoch; while the one who died and did not decay was Lot's wife turned into a pillar of salt for the seasoning of such insipid minds as yours that strut so stupidly.'

Monasticism flourished in Egypt from the time of its foundation by Pachomius. Monks belonging to the same trade were lodged together in one house under a superior; for example, weavers in one and mat-makers in another. Since most of the monks spoke Coptic, an Alexandrian who spent three years as a novice in one of the Pachomian monasteries in the 350s was assigned to the Greek house where the small group of Greek speakers lived.

Each Easter and on 13 August ('Founder's Day'?), there was a general assembly of all the monks from the Pachomian monasteries at the original house at Tabennisi. In Jerome's day (about AD 390), nearly 50,000 monks would gather to celebrate Easter.

4 Athanasius

Pachomius had a friend who lived 400 miles north in Alexandria. His name was Athanasius, a great upholder of the Christian faith. At one point in his career, it even seemed as if Athanasius stood alone for the truth of the gospel against the whole world. From time to time, Athanasius had to flee for his life. On at least one such occasion, he found refuge amongst the monasteries founded by Pachomius.

Athanasius was a very important person in the Church in Egypt in the fourth century. He became Bishop or Patriarch of Alexandria in AD 328. In AD 367 he wrote his thirty-ninth *Easter Letter* (**1.9**). In this, he defined for the very first time what has come to be known as the canon of the New Testament. He drew up a list of books that he considered to be suitable reading for Christians – the twenty-seven books now in our New Testament. These – and only these – should be read in services of public worship, though a few others could be read by catechumens. These others included the *Didache* (*Teaching of the Apostles*) and the *Shepherd of Hermas*. All others were banned. The purpose of Athanasius in making such a compilation was to exclude from the reading list of Christians the large number of apocryphal books. These were being read, and to a great extent composed, by Christians in Egypt.

5 Monastic Library Purge

It would appear that some of the monks in the Pachomian monasteries had been reading – perhaps even composing or copying by hand – some of these banned books. In AD 367, Theodore, who had succeeded Pachomius as head of the monastery at Tabennisi and presumably as abbot-general of the other monasteries, ordained that the thirty-ninth *Easter Letter* of Athanasius should be translated into Coptic, the language of the majority of the monks, and should be read in all the Pachomian monasteries of the region of the southern Thebaid. He felt that this letter was justly aimed against books that were being spuriously concocted by heretics and to which they were attributing antiquity by giving them the names of the apostles.

It is possible that this letter and its translation into Coptic led to a purge of monastic libraries in the southern Thebaid. There is evidence of such censorship of books even during the lifetime of Pachomius. On one occasion, it was revealed to him that some hermits who had come to visit him had read the writings of Origen, which he considered heretical. He ordered them to take all Origen's books in their possession and 'throw them into the river and never want to read them again, especially the blasphemous ones'.[6]

There may have been a similar censorship of books following Athanasius' thirty-ninth *Easter Letter* and its translation into Coptic. Instead of burning the banned books or throwing them into the River Nile, the monks at Chenoboskion apparently decided to bury twelve bound volumes in a clay jar. Such receptacles were less costly than cupboards and were often used for storing books and other valuables. It was in such jars that the Dead Sea Scrolls were discovered. Jeremiah also was told to put the title-deeds for the field that he purchased at Anathoth in an earthenware vessel to preserve them (Jeremiah 32.14). The monks chose a disused cemetery some two-and-a-half miles from Chenoboskion as their hiding place. There they placed the precious jar of books amongst chalky cliffs overlooking the River Nile. There they lay hidden for nearly 1,600 years.

The contents of the codices show that the monks who copied,

read and hid them were not just adherents of a gnostic sect who, for some reason or other, joined a Christian monastery. Rather, they were ascetics who were interested in reading books containing strange views. It is not surprising that such people should be found in the monasteries. These were not so much strongholds of true doctrine but of correct practice, including strict asceticism, humility and obedience. Orthodoxy (correct opinion) was important only in so far as it affected relations with the Patriarch of Alexandria, under whose jurisdiction the monks ultimately fell.[7]

There is another piece of evidence connecting these old books with fourth-century Coptic monks. Waste papyrus that was used to pack and to strengthen the covers of the codices contain old Greek and Coptic letters and receipts. Some of these indicate a monastic background and are dated to the first half of the fourth century. For example, two papyrus fragments dated AD 341 and 346 contain receipts and there is a deed of surety that can be dated to 348. This suggests that the codices were bound together in the latter half of the fourth century. Not only so; but three of the covers included documents with parts of the name Chenoboskion written on them. The Greek word *Chenoboskites* (an inhabitant of Chenoboskion) appears as part of the address on the back of a fragmentary letter within the cover of the volume containing the *Gospel of Thomas*.[8]

Of course, the fact that the covers were manufactured in a Pachomian monastery does not necessarily mean that the books belonged to a monastic library. The monks could have bound the codices for an individual customer or for a group of people outside the monastery. Yet it seems more likely that they were for use within the monastery itself. Even so, they could have been kept by the monks, not because the monks sympathized with the heretical teaching contained in them but because they wished to know enough about the heresies to be able to refute them. They might have buried them after they had finished with them so that they would not corrupt unsuspecting readers. However, it is probably more likely that the monks read them for their own edification. The books do not really form a library as such. They are a collection of books of various kinds produced and used by different individuals. They are certainly not the standardized products of a monastic scriptorium. Only a few of them are heretical. Some are even pagan.

6 Character of Pachomian Monasteries

This view can be further supported by consideration of the character of the Pachomian monasteries themselves. A Christian with gnostic leanings would not have been excluded from membership of one of these communities. In the early years of the Pachomian monasteries, Pachomius received under his care monasteries not originally founded by him. There is no evidence that he tested the orthodoxy of the monks before accepting their institutions into his jurisdiction. In fact, we read of the burial of a bad monk at whose funeral Pachomius refused to allow psalms to be sung or the Eucharist to be celebrated. Then he collected the dead monk's clothes and burned them.[9]

7 Conclusion

It seems clear that the Nag Hammadi codices were not, after all, part of a gnostic library. They did not belong to a group of gnostic heretics living together in Egypt who, for some unknown reason, decided to hide their precious books in chalky cliffs overlooking the River Nile. The books belonged rather to Coptic monks living in some of the Pachomian monasteries in the Thebaid. In particular, some – if not all – of the owners of this hidden treasure were resident in the Pachomian monastery at Chenoboskion, on the other side of the river from the village of Nag Hammadi. The occasion of their burial of this load of old books was a purge of their monastic library following upon the publication of Athanasius' thirty-ninth *Easter Letter* and its translation into Coptic by order of Theodore, successor of Pachomius as abbot-general.

Part Three

The Coptic Gospel of Thomas

CHAPTER EIGHT

Not Another Gospel

1 Coptic *Gospel of Thomas*

The second codex found in the jar at Chenoboskion is the finest volume in the whole remarkable collection. It contains seven works, the second of which is the *Gospel of Thomas*.[1] This document takes up twenty pages of manuscript. It begins: 'These are the hidden sayings which the living Jesus spoke and Didymus Judas Thomas wrote.' Appended to the work is the title by which it has come to be known: 'The Gospel according to Thomas'.

2 Not a Gospel

One of the first things to be said about *Thomas* is that it is not a gospel in the normally accepted sense of the word, in spite of its appended title. It is totally unlike the four canonical gospels – Matthew, Mark, Luke and John. It contains little or no narrative. The nearest we get to narrative is in the opening words of a few sayings, such as *Thomas* 22a: 'Jesus saw children who were being suckled' (10.25); *Thomas* 60: 'They saw a Samaritan carrying a lamb on his way to Judaea' (10.33); *Thomas* 100: 'They showed Jesus a gold coin' (12.29). There are narrative elements within *Thomas* 13: 'Jesus departed and spoke three words to Thomas. When Thomas came to his companions, they asked him: . . .' (12.2). There is no record of the birth, life, death and resurrection of Jesus of Nazareth. It comprises simply 114 composite sayings allegedly spoken by the living Jesus (**10.1**) and written down by Didymus Judas Thomas.

This Coptic *Gospel of Thomas* has to be carefully distinguished from another book with the same name, the *Infancy Gospel of Thomas* (13.2). This latter contains fanciful stories about the boy Jesus between the ages of five and twelve years. Cyril, Bishop of Jerusalem in the fourth century, warned Christians not to read this book.

3 Biblical Parallels and Echoes

As can be seen from Table 1, of the 114 sayings in the Coptic *Gospel of Thomas*, 66 have parallels or echoes in the synoptic gospels, those in Matthew and Luke predominating over those in Mark (59 in Matthew, 18 in Mark, 46 in Luke), while another 12 of them have echoes in the Fourth Gospel.[2] Altogether, 32 sayings contain phrases reminiscent of words spoken by Jesus according to John's Gospel. In addition, there are 6 sayings containing echoes of other parts of the New Testament and 9 with Old Testament references. Only 30 out of the 114 sayings in the *Gospel of Thomas* seem to have no biblical echoes.

Table 1 Biblical Parallels and Echoes in *Thomas*						
Thomas	Matthew	Mark	Luke	John	Rest NT	OT
66	59	18	46	10	15	7
12	0	0	0	22	5	1
6	0	0	0	0	6	1
30	0	0	0	0	0	0
114	59	18	46	32	26	9

4 Parables

Included in these 114 sayings are 15 parables (9.2) of which 12[3] are found in the canonical gospels, while 3 are completely new. Of the 12 with synoptic parallels, 3 are from Mark, 4 are from Q (though there may have been versions of 2 of these also in M – the parables of the marriage feast and the lost sheep), 4 are from M and 1 is from L (3.2) (see Table 2 – 9.2).

5 Beatitudes

There are 13 beatitudes in *Thomas* (**9.3**), 12 ascribed to Jesus. Ten of them begin: 'Jesus said: "Happy are / is . . .".' Some of these beatitudes are quite unlike anything found in the canonical gospels. The majority, however, have parallels in the New Testament. There are 3 beatitudes in *Thomas* 79 (9.25, 26), but the first is not included in this book since it was uttered by a woman in the crowd (see chapter 18, note 3).

6 Catchwords

For the rest, there are proverbial sayings, epigrams and aphorisms. Some of these seem to have been arranged on the basis of catchwords.[4] For example, *Thomas* 2 (10.2) and 3 (10.24) have in common the root idea of reigning, since the abstract noun for kingdom in *Thomas* 3 is related to the verb in *Thomas* 2. The 2 sayings in *Thomas* 5 (10.32) are linked by the double occurrence of the syllable meaning 'hidden'. The idea of revelation links 2 sayings within *Thomas* 6 (10.17). *Thomas* 7 (9.16) and *Thomas* 8 (9.1) are connected by 'man'. In *Thomas* 8 (9.1), *Thomas* 9 (9.2) and *Thomas* 10 (11.10), the same verb is used of the fisherman casting his net and also throwing all the small fish into the sea, of the sower scattering his seed and of Jesus casting fire upon the earth. *Thomas* 12 (12.1) and 13 (12.2) have 'righteous' in common. *Thomas* 25 (12.12) and 26 (12.13) are doubly linked with 'brother' and 'eye'.

7 Introductions

Each of the 114 sayings is introduced by one of the following introductory formulae: 'Jesus said'; 'He said'; 'And he said'; 'Jesus said to them'; 'Jesus said to his disciples'. In certain cases, these introductory words are preceded by a preliminary question asked by the disciples or by Mary or by Salome; a request from the disciples or from a man; a statement made by the disciples or by one of them – Simon Peter, or by a woman in the crowd.

8 Sayings Collection

The predominance of sayings with parallels in Matthew and Luke suggests one of several possibilities: either the compiler of *Thomas* used Matthew and Luke as we know them; or he used the same sources (Q, M and L); or he used another sayings collection or collections like Q or M or L; or *Thomas* in its original form and language was itself a collection of sayings of Jesus gathered from the common oral tradition on which all such sayings collections ultimately depend (**3.2**). This is the most likely of all the alternatives. *Thomas* is not a gospel in the same sense as the canonical gospels but a loosely connected collection of sayings attributed to the living Jesus. It belongs to the same literary type as the hypothetical document known as Q, the common source behind the gospels of Matthew and Luke (**3.2**).[5]

9 Independence of Synoptics

Ever since the discovery of this collection of sayings, there has been controversy with regard to its independence or otherwise of the synoptic gospels. Scholars seem to be fairly evenly divided on this matter.

As long ago as 1958, Johannes von Leipoldt was convinced that we can gain from the *Gospel of Thomas* an insight into the tradition underlying the synoptic gospels that is independent of them. In certain cases, the text of *Thomas* leads us back to the oldest tradition.[6]

About the same time, Gilles Quispel, Professor of the History of Religion at the University of Utrecht, wrote: 'It seems to me that this discovery is much more important than even the wildest reporters dream of, if only we are willing to apply the methods of scholarship. The importance of the *Gospel of Thomas* lies in the fact that it contains independent and very old gospel tradition.'[7]

In a book published in 1993, Stephen Patterson argued from a careful study of both the content and the order of the sayings in this document that there is no evidence to suggest that *Thomas* is dependent upon the synoptic texts.[8]

The controversy, however, continues. In his latest book, Graham Stanton declares that scholars defending either of the two views, dependence or independence, 'often sound like politicians: they claim that they represent majority opinion, and they largely ignore the strongest points made by their opponents. The issues at stake are important, complex and fascinating.' Stanton himself seems to come out in the end on the side of those who believe that *Thomas* was dependent on the canonical gospels, to a certain extent at least. 'While it is just possible that Thomas drew solely on many strands of oral traditions from diverse branches of earliest Christianity, it is perhaps more likely that some traditions have been drawn from the canonical gospels.'[9]

I myself believe that the Coptic *Gospel of Thomas* may be independent of the canonical gospels and that it contains authentic sayings of Jesus.

10 Original Language

The original language of the *Gospel of Thomas* may have been Aramaic, the language which Jesus probably used most of the time. It is more likely that it was first compiled in Syriac, a dialect of Aramaic spoken in Edessa and its province. There are good reasons for believing that it originated in Syria, perhaps in or around Edessa, the cradle of Syriac-speaking Christianity.[10]

11 Thomas and Edessa

Christianity probably reached Edessa before the end of the first century, even though the first sure evidence of its presence belongs to about a century later. From early times, the apostle associated with the spread of Christianity to this area was Thomas. According to tradition, it was he who sent Thaddaeus to Syria in response to a request for help from Abgar the Great (13.3). Thomas himself is said to have preached the gospel in India, but there is a church dedicated to him in Edessa and his body was believed to have been brought there from India by a merchant in AD 394.

12 Whose Twin was Thomas?

In the Preface to the Coptic *Gospel of Thomas*, the apostle is referred to as Didymus Judas Thomas. In the New Testament, on the other hand, he is referred to on three occasions as Thomas called Didymus (John 11.16; 20.24; 21.2) – Thomas being a transliteration into Greek of the Aramaic *toma* ('twin'). In the RSV the whole phrase is translated as, 'Thomas called the Twin'. However, in the works of the Eastern Church Fathers, especially those writing in Syriac, Thomas is regularly called Judas Thomas. There seems to be no doubt that his real name was Judas. He was called Thomas ('twin'), for which the Greek word was *Didymus*, to distinguish him from other apostles bearing the same name. In the East, he still retained his original name and was referred to as Judas Thomas ('Judas the Twin').

Old Syriac versions of the four gospels dating from the fourth century testify to variant readings at John 14.22. Instead of 'Judas (not Iscariot) said to him . . .', they read either 'Judas Thomas' or 'Thomas said to him . . .'.

But whose twin was he? The apocryphal *Acts of Thomas*, which appears to be dependent on the *Gospel of Thomas* and was composed in Syriac in or near Edessa in the first half of the third century, describes him as Judas Thomas Didymus. He is even said to be 'twin brother of Christ'. The one is mistaken for the other. It is little wonder that, in some manuscripts of the *Acts of Thomas*, this title is obliterated. No orthodox circle of Christians would wish to develop and pass on this remarkable belief that Thomas was the twin brother of Jesus. In the closely related *Book of Thomas the Contender*, also composed in Syria during the first half of the third century, Thomas is called Judas Thomas.

13 Tatian's *Gospel Harmony*

Further evidence for the Syrian origin of the *Gospel of Thomas* can be deduced from the writings of the Syrian Christian called Tatian. About AD 170, Tatian produced a unified account (or harmony) of the ministry of Jesus by putting together, either in Greek or in Syriac, the four gospels. This was known as the *Diatessaron* ('through four') and was the standard text of the gospels in the Syriac-speaking churches till the seventh century.[11]

It is possible that Tatian used not only the four canonical gospels for the compilation of his *Diatessaron* but also a fifth source. The title ('through four') could be explained by the picture of five separate columns providing only four separate entrances: O X O X O X O X O – where O represents a column (i.e., one of Tatian's five sources) and X represents an entrance. The fact that, in the sixth century, Victor of Capua referred to the *Diatessaron* as *Diapente* ('through five') could be taken as support for Tatian's use of five sources. Another suggestion is that 'through four' and 'through five' are simply musical terms referring respectively to three intervals of four notes and four intervals of five notes. This seems too complicated and rather far-fetched.

If we can accept the view that Tatian used five sources instead of four, then his fifth source might have been the *Gospel of the Hebrews*) (**15.4**),[12] only fragments of which have survived as quotations in early writers, or it could have been the *Gospel of Thomas*. This would account for the many parallels that exist between Tatian's *Diatessaron* and *Thomas*.[13]

14 The Church in Edessa

But what was the character of early Syriac Christianity? Documents associated with eastern Syria include not only the *Diatessaron*, and the *Acts of Thomas*, but also the *Book of Thomas the Contender* and the *Odes of Solomon*.[14] All these writings contain an extreme asceticism known as encratism, from the Greek word meaning 'self-control', also to be found in the Coptic *Gospel of Thomas* (**3.10**). One of the main doctrines taught was that the Christian life was unobtainable except by those who were celibate. In fact, baptism was reserved in the first few centuries in the Syrian Church for those who led an ascetic life. One document makes it quite clear that only celibates were worthy of receiving the kingdom and becoming full members of the Church. All others were only companions or adherents.[15] There are several sayings in the Coptic *Gospel of Thomas* that give the same impression, as we shall see in the next chapter.

15 How Gnostic is *Thomas*?

From the time of its discovery, it was taken for granted that the Coptic *Gospel of Thomas* was gnostic through and through.[16] It was therefore assumed that we could not expect to find any authentic sayings of Jesus accurately reproduced in it. However, there were no gnostics at Edessa in the first or early second century. Any so-called gnostic sayings in *Thomas* appear to bear the hallmarks of encratism. This would account for its extreme asceticism.[17]

16 Solitary One

This is seen in particular in those sayings in *Thomas* which contain the Greek word *monachos* – *Thomas* 16 (11.11); 49 (9.19); 75 (12.8). Originally an adjective meaning 'single' or 'solitary', it is used here for the first time in literature as a noun meaning 'solitary one'[18] It is the word that came to be used for a monk, hence the English word.

A few years ago, the Greek word came to light in a petition from an Egyptian peasant dated 6 June 324. He complains that his neighbours' cow had eaten his crops. He had caught the cow and was leading it to the village when his neighbours attacked him with a big club. He was rescued from death by a deacon and a monk by the name of Isaac. This is the earliest occurrence of the Greek word *monachos* in the sense of 'monk'.[19]

17 Single One

In *Thomas*, *monachos* is used as the equivalent of the Coptic expression *oua ouot* ('single one') – *Thomas* 4 (10.27); *Thomas* 22b (10.26); *Thomas* 23 (12.6). The only other place where a parallel term occurs is in Syriac literature associated with Edessa and its surrounding area.

The *monachos* in *Thomas* is clearly someone who is beyond sexuality. He is like a little child (*Thomas* 22a – 10.25), whose innocence of sexuality is such that he can remove his clothes without shame (*Thomas* 21a – 9.4; *Thomas* 37 – 12.7). The promise of entering the bridal chamber reserved for those who have renounced marriage (*Thomas* 75 – 12.8) reminds one of the situation in the early Syrian Church. This is not gnosticism but encratism. As such, it carries one stage further than the canonical gospels the sayings of Jesus about detaching oneself from the world, abandoning possessions and leaving one's wife and family in order to follow him (Matthew 6.19; 6.24; 8.20; Mark 8.34; 10.21, 23; Luke 14.26). If we can separate such encratitic sayings from others in *Thomas* we may be left with authentic gold. Here we enter the realm of redaction criticism (**3.4**), assessing the contribution of the person or persons who composed the document. As we turn to consider in the following four chapters all the sayings attributed to Jesus in the Coptic *Gospel of Thomas*, we shall grade as D (of doubtful authenticity) those bearing the encratitic mark.

CHAPTER NINE

Parables and Beatitudes

1 Progress so far

With this chapter, we return to our study of actual sayings attributed to Jesus. This was started in chapter 4 with our consideration of words of the Lord within the New Testament but outside the four gospels and also of a few found in later manuscripts of the gospels. In chapters 5 and 6, we studied scraps of old paper from Egyptian rubbish dumps. Chapter 7 may appear to some as an interlude on the origins of monasticism, but was intended to set the scene for the discovery of the load of old books at Chenoboskion and to suggest the possible non-gnostic character of the Coptic *Gospel of Thomas*. In chapter 8, we looked at this amazing document as a whole and considered its independence or otherwise of the synoptic gospels, original language, place of origin and some of its characteristics. Now we are ready to examine the sayings in *Thomas*.

2 Parables

Apart from catchwords (**8.6**), there seems to be little reason for the arrangement of sayings within the Coptic *Gospel of Thomas*. However, there are clearly identifiable types which can be classified and studied together. In this chapter, we shall be looking at parables and beatitudes. In chapters 10 to 12, sayings will be classified according to content rather than form, as here.[1]

There are 15 parables (**8.4**), of which 12 are already known to us from Matthew, Mark and Luke. Three are completely new. Since they are not attested elsewhere, 2 of these have been graded C and one D. In the following table, the probable sources from which the synoptic evangelists drew their versions are also indicated – Q, M, L and Mark (**3.2**; **8.4**). The versions found in *Thomas* may well be independent of the synoptic gospels and of their sources (**8.9**).[2]

Ref.	Parable	Thomas No.	Matthew	Mark	Luke	Gospel Source	Grade
9.1	Wise Fisherman	8	13.47–50				A
9.2	Sower	9	13.3–9	4.3–9	8.5–8	Mark	A
9.3	Mustard seed	20	13.31f.	4.30–32	13.18f.	Mark Q	A
9.4	Children	21a					D
9.5	Householder	21b	24.43		12.39	Q	B
9.6	Weed	57	13.24–30			M	A
9.7	Rich man	63			12.16–21	L	A
9.8	Guests	64	22.1–10		14.15–24	Q/M	A
9.9	Vineyard	65	21.33–46	12.1–12	20.9–19	Mark	A
9.10	Pearl	76	13.45f.			M	A
9.11	Leaven	96	13.33		13.20	Q	A
9.12	Jar of Meal	97					C
9.13	Assassin	98					C
9.14	Lost Sheep	107	18.12–14		15.4–7	Q/M	A
9.15	Hidden Treasure	109	13.44			M	C

Table 2
Parables in *Thomas*

9.1 – Thomas 8   A

The man is like a wise fisherman
who cast his net into the sea.
He drew it up from the sea
full of small fish.
Among them he found a large, beautiful fish.
That wise fisherman

> *threw all the small fish into the sea.*
> *He chose the large fish without regret.*
> *Let whoever has ears to hear, hear.*

This version of the parable of the dragnet (Matthew 13.47–50) points to more authentic tradition.[3] In the second century, Tatian (**8.13**) and Clement of Alexandria (**16.6**) knew a similar version. Here in *Thomas*, the parable opens with 'The man is like . . .' instead of 'The kingdom is like . . .'. The 'man' has been substituted for 'kingdom' either to link it up by means of a catchword with the previous saying (*Thomas* 7 – 9.16) or as a reference to Jesus.[4] The parable is about one fisherman, as in Tatian and Clement, whereas Matthew 13.48 refers to 'the men'. In all three non-canonical versions, it is a casting-net that is being used rather than a dragnet (Matthew 13.47). There was nothing particularly wise in discarding all the small fish. Could he not have kept them all? The choice of the large fish need not imply the gnostic's choice of the true or divine self.[5] It stresses the point of the parable – the joy of a great discovery – not the mixture of people in the kingdom of heaven (Matthew 13.47). So he chose the one fish without regret. The refrain – 'Let whoever has ears to hear, hear' – is found frequently in *Thomas*, but never attached to any parable with which it is associated in the canonical gospels. In this respect, *Thomas* is a law to itself.

9.2 – Thomas 9 A

> *See, the sower went out.*
> *He scattered a handful of seed,*
> *Some seed fell upon the road;*
> *the birds came and gathered them up.*
> *Others fell upon the rock,*
> *did not take root in the soil*
> *and did not send ears up to heaven.*
> *And others fell upon the thorns;*
> *they choked the seed and the worm ate them.*
> *And others fell upon the good soil*

> ***and sent good fruit up to heaven***
> ***sixtyfold and one hundred and twentyfold.***

This version, unlike those in Matthew 13.3–9 and Luke 8.5–8, is
not based on Mark 4.3–9. The shortest versions of the parable
are those in Luke and in *Thomas*. In his section about the rocky
ground, Luke has cut down on the repetitious language of Mark.
Yet *Thomas* is not dependent on Luke 8.5–8, since it differs
radically about the reason for the failure of these seed. *Thomas* 9
may bear witness to the original length of this section of the
parable and therefore of the whole parable. As far as content is
concerned, the version of *Thomas* is less awkward than those in
the synoptic gospels and makes better agricultural sense.[6]

The most important variant reading is 'upon the road' – not
'beside the road'. The Aramaic phrase could signify either.[7]
Thomas has chosen the more correct meaning and makes better
agricultural sense. Yet how the worm could eat up the seed sown
among thorns if they had already been choked is a mystery.

The absence of the allegorical interpretation found in all
three synoptic gospels confirms the view that it was the work of
the early Church though it may well be true to the mind of Jesus.

9.3 – Thomas 20 A

> *The kingdom of heaven is like a mustard seed*
> *smaller than all seeds*
> *but when it falls upon the tilled earth*
> *it produces large branches*
> *and becomes shelter for the birds of heaven.*

Mustard was very common in Palestine, being cultivated in
fields, not gardens (as in Luke 13.19). Its seed was proverbial for
its smallness. A common rabbinic proverb spoke of a tiny
quantity of something as being like to a grain of mustard.
According to a present-day Arab proverb: 'No mustard seed slips
from the hands of a miser.'

In Matthew 13.31–33 and Luke 13.18–21 but not Mark 4.30–
32, the parable is paired with that of the leaven (*Thomas* 96 –

9.11), not found in Mark. They may have appeared together in Q, therefore. The fact that they are separated in *Thomas* may indicate that Jesus told them on different occasions and also that *Thomas* is both early and independent of Q.

The tilled earth is not necessarily the prepared soil of the true gnostic, as some have suggested. It may have been an integral part of the original parable.[8]

The large branches correspond to the large branches in Mark 4.32 and to large loaves in *Thomas* 96 (9.11). The shelter for the birds of heaven is also similar to the version in Mark 4.32.

9.4 – Thomas *21a*   D

They are like little children
who have installed themselves in a field
which is not theirs.
When the owners of the field come, they will say:
'Release to us our field.'
They take off their clothes before them
to release the field and give it back to them.

In response to a question from Mary, 'Whom are your disciples like?', Jesus tells this strange parable. Mary appears again in *Thomas* 114 (12.10), but in neither case is she further identified. 'The field' is the world, as in Matthew 13.38. For the idea of the temporary residence of Christians in a world that does not belong to them, compare Peter's description of his readers as aliens and exiles (1 Peter 2.11). Jesus himself said to his disciples: 'You are not of this world' (John 15.19). Compare 1 Corinthians 7.31 – 'The form of this world is passing away'; *Thomas* 42 – 'Become passers by' (12.20); the Arabic bridge saying (17.30). The coming of the owners of the field refers to the coming of death, which is likened to taking off one's clothes. Paul, on the other hand, sees death as putting on heavenly clothes over the earthly so that we may not be found naked (2 Corinthians 5.3).[9]

9.5 – Thomas *21b* B

If the householder knows
that the thief is coming
he will stay awake before he comes
and will not let him dig through
into his house of the kingdom
to carry away his goods.
You then must watch for the world.
Gird up your loins with great strength
lest the robbers find a way to come to you
and gain the advantage over you.
Let there be among you a person of understanding.
When the fruit ripened he came quickly
with his sickle in his hand and reaped it.
Let whoever has ears to hear, hear.

In further response to Mary's question (*Thomas* 21a – 9.4), Jesus
tells another parable, found also in Matthew 24.43 and Luke
12.39 (Q). There it is found in the past tense as if Jesus had in
mind one such incident that had recently occurred.[10] It
reappears in *Thomas* 103 (9.27) as a beatitude, where the
happy person knows in which part of the night the robbers will
break in. In *Thomas* 21b, the parable is followed by exhortations
to watchfulness and to preparedness, by a call to understanding,
by an echo of the parable growing secretly (Mark 4.29), and by
an exhortation to effective hearing. Since most of the
components of this composite saying can be paralleled in the
New Testament, it is likely that Jesus gave expression to these
sentiments, though not necessarily in this form.

9.6 – Thomas 57 A

The kingdom of the Father is like
a man who had good seed.
His enemy came by night.
He sowed a weed among the good seed.
The man did not permit them to pull up the weed.

> *He said to them:*
> *'Lest perhaps you go to pull up the weed*
> *and pull up the wheat with it.'*
> *For on the day of harvest the weeds will appear.*
> *They will pull them up and burn them.*

In the New Testament, the parable of the weeds (in the plural) is found only in Matthew 13.24–30, with an allegorical interpretation in Matthew 13.37–43. It is paired with the parable of the dragnet (Matthew 13.47–50). In Matthew, Jesus is warning against premature weeding and teaching that the separation of the good from the bad should be left to God on Judgement Day. In *Thomas*, the emphasis falls on the pulling up and burning of the weeds on the day of harvest. For the time being, good and evil coexist side by side.

9.7 – Thomas 63 A

> *There was a rich man who had much money.*
> *He said: 'I will use my money*
> *so that I may sow and reap and plant*
> *and fill my storehouses with fruit*
> *so that I lack nothing.*
> *This is what he thought in his heart.*
> *And that night he died.*
> *Let whoever has ears, hear.*

In spite of several differences from Luke 12.16–21, this is simply a different version of the same parable. The lesson in both is that worldly wealth offers no lasting security. The preceding verses in Luke (Luke 12.13–15), which give the context, are not found in *Thomas* till *Thomas* 72 (11.12). This suggests that it was Luke or his source that put the saying into that context.

9.8 – Thomas 64 A

A man had guests.
When he had prepared dinner
he sent his servant to summon the guests.
He went to the first and said to him:
'My master summons you.'
He said: 'I have some money due to me
from some merchants.
They are about to come to me this evening.
I shall go and set out supplies for them.
I pray to be excused from the dinner.'
He went to another and said to him:
'My master invited you.'
He said to him: 'I have bought a house
and they request me for a day.
I will have no time.'
He came to another and said to him:
'My master summons you.'
He said to him: 'My friend is to be married
and I am to arrange a dinner.
I shall not be able to come.
I pray to be excused from the dinner.'
He went to another and said to him:
'My master summons you.'
He said to him: 'I have bought a village
and I go to collect the rent.
I shall not be able to come.
I pray to be excused.'
The servant came and said to his master:
'Those whom you invited to the dinner
have excused themselves.'
The master said to him: 'Go out to the roads,
bring those whom you shall find
so that they may dine.'

**Tradesmen and merchants shall not enter
the places of my Father.**

This is an independent version of the Q (**3.2**) parable of the great
supper found in Luke 14.15–24. The version in Matthew 22.1–10,
the marriage of the king's son, is an allegorization of the Q
parable in the light of the destruction of Jerusalem in AD 70.
Thomas 64 gives no hint of this reinterpretation. It omits the
reference to the violence done to the king's servants (Matthew
22.6), the angry retaliation of the king (Matthew 22.7), and the
rejection of the guest without a wedding garment (Matthew
22.11–14). It is closer to the version in Luke 14.15–24; but even
Luke is not free from allegorization. He has introduced two search
parties to match the Jewish and Gentile missions of the church
(Luke 14.21–23). He has also added verse 24: 'For I tell you, none
of those men who were invited shall taste my banquet.'

Thomas 64 is devoid of allegorizing details but is ingenious in
elaborating the excuses: the guests had legitimate business to do.
It is quite clear that the version in *Thomas* is independent of
those in Matthew and Luke. It may contain authentic touches,
though the assumption that businessmen fall short of perfection
may be due to the origin of *Thomas* in the encratite community
at Edessa. Furthermore, since the traditional number in folk-tales
is three, it is possible that one of the four excuses has been added
in the course of transmission, though which is uncertain.[11]

9.9 – Thomas 65   A

*A good man had a vineyard.
He gave it to tenants so that they would work it
and that he would receive its fruit.
He sent his servant to them
so that the tenants would give him
the fruit of the vineyard.
They seized the servant and beat him.
A little longer and they would have killed him.
The servant came and told his master.
His master said: 'Perhaps he did not know them.'*

> *He sent another servant.*
> *The tenants beat him as well.*
> *Then the owner sent his son.*
> *He said: 'Perhaps they will respect my son.'*
> *Since those tenants knew*
> *that he was the heir of the vineyard*
> *they seized him and killed him.*
> *Let whoever has ears to hear, hear.*

This version is much shorter than that in the synoptic gospels (Matthew 21.33–36; Mark 12.1–12; Luke 20.9–19) and contains little, if any, allegory.[12] In this respect, as in others, it is closest to Luke 20.9–19. The man is good, possibly because between the sending of the first and second servants he gave the tenants the benefit of the doubt. If he did not know them, they would not know who he was. Possible authentic touches include omission of any reference to the second coming of Jesus and the reservation of the killing to the owner's son. In its original form, the parable may have had two servants before the son – a climactic series of three characteristic of folk-tales.[13] Moreover, the simplicity of the description of murder amongst the vines is to be preferred to the more elaborate synoptic versions. The closing refrain is unique, as usual, to *Thomas*.[14]

9.10 – Thomas 76 A

> *The kingdom of the Father is like*
> *a merchant who had merchandise and found a pearl.*
> *This merchant was a wise man.*
> *He sold the merchandise*
> *and bought the pearl for himself.*
> *Seek for the treasure which fails not*
> *which endures where no moth comes near to devour*
> *and no worm destroys.*

Instead of 'a merchant in search of fine pearls' (Matthew 13.45), *Thomas* has a general merchant, which may be more primitive.[15]

Again, it is not 'one pearl of great value' (Matthew 13.46) that Jesus is talking about, but just an ordinary pearl. Any pearl has a certain value for someone who is not a pearl merchant. In order to gain it, this wise man 'sold the mrchandise' rather than 'all that he had' (Matthew 13.46), which would not have been a wise thing to do.[16] To this parable *Thomas* adds the saying about treasure found also in Q (Matthew 6.20; Luke 12.33). In Matthew, the parable of the pearl (Matthew 13.45f.) is preceded by the parable of the hidden treasure (Matthew 13.44), which is found in *Thomas* 109 (9.15). Taken over all, the version of the parable in *Thomas* 76 is more easily understood than those in the synoptic gospels.

9.11 – Thomas 96 A

**The kingdom of the Father is like a woman
who has taken a little leaven
and has hidden it in dough
and has made large loaves of it.
Let whoever has ears to hear, hear.**

In both Matthew 13.33 and Luke 13.20f., the parable of the leaven is paired with that of the mustard seed found in *Thomas* 20 (9.3). As in four other parables in *Thomas* – *Thomas* 8 (9.1); 97 (9.12); 98 (9.13); 109 (9.15) – the kingdom is compared to a person rather than to a thing (such as leaven) or an event.[17] It could well be that more of the parables of Jesus originally began with a comparison with a person or with the action of people in certain circumstances.[18] Here, the fact that the subject is a woman may vouch for its authenticity, considering the patriarchal nature of society in those days.[19]

The adjective 'little' is missing from the version of the parable in Matthew and Luke, but it is found in two Pauline passages (1 Corinthians 5.6; Galatians 5.9) and is absolutely necessary to a proper understanding of the parable: the contrast between the smallness of the leaven and the greatness of the resulting loaves.[20]

In the Q version of the parable, the woman took and hid the

leaven in three measures of flour, which is a ridiculously large amount – 'half a hundredweight' (NEB) – sufficient to feed about 160 people.[21] Perhaps Q has been influenced by the amount given in Genesis 18.6.

In several small details – the comparison with a person, the addition of 'little' and 'large', the omission of the weight of flour – *Thomas* 96 seems to preserve a better version of the parable of the leaven than do Matthew and Luke. In addition, the version in *Thomas* seems also to have been known to Paul, who has some of these details in 1 Corinthians 5.6 and Galatians 5.9. *Thomas* and Paul, therefore, point to common tradition with regard to this parable that is independent of the synoptic gospels.[22]

9.12 – Thomas 97   c

The kingdom of the Father is like a woman
who was carrying a jar full of meal.
While she was walking on a distant road,
the handle of the jar broke.
the meal streamed out behind her on the road.
She did not know it
since she had not noticed the accident.
After she came into the house,
she put the jar down and found it empty.

Since this homely parable of the broken jar or the careless woman is found nowhere else it has to be graded C. However, it could be authentic.[23] It cannot be dismissed as a gnostic fabrication since it would be difficult to imagine gnostics making up a story whose subject was a woman.

What is the meaning of this parable? It could be a warning against Christian self-assurance and lack of watchfulness.[24] It has been pointed out that the parables on either side of it – the woman baking large loaves and the man slaying a powerful man – emphasize a person's ability to succeed, while the woman alone on a distant road fails to arrive at her destination with a jar full of meal. This tension between the parables could convey the meaning of this one, namely, that on one's own a person cannot be successful.[25] If so, the message could be that divine help is required in the Christian life, as Paul realized: 'I can do all things through him who strengthens me' (Philippians 4.13).

9.13 – Thomas 98   c

The kingdom of the Father is like a man
who wishes to kill a powerful man.
He drew the sword in his house
and stuck it into the wall
in order to know
whether his hand would carry through.
Then he slew the powerful man.

This previously unknown parable teaches a similar lesson to the parables of the tower builder (Luke 14.28–30) and the king going to war (Luke 14.31f.) They are vivid pictures of men from very different walks of life who wish to prepare themselves realistically for the responsibility they assume. So Jesus demands self-testing and counting of the cost before setting out on the Christian life. The use of an immoral deed as an example does not militate against the authenticity of the parable. Jesus also told a story about a dishonest steward (Luke 16.1–8).[26]

9.14 – Thomas 107   a

The kingdom is like a shepherd
who had a hundred sheep.
One of them, the largest, went astray.
He left behind the ninety-nine
and sought after the one until he found it.
Having tired himself out, he said to the sheep:
'I love you more than ninety-nine.'

In the New Testament, there are two versions of this parable – Matthew 18.12–14 (M or Q) and Luke 15.4–7 (L or Q). The discrepancies between them make it unlikely that they were derived from the same source.[27] Neither version begins like *Thomas* 107. By referring to 'a shepherd' rather than to 'a man', *Thomas* has strong echoes of Ezekiel 34.16, where God is the shepherd who promises to watch over 'the fat and the strong', a reference to Israel. So this parable in *Thomas* is about the divine election or choice of Israel, which is a constant theme in both the Old and the New Testament.[28] This may be closer to the original meaning of the parable as told by Jesus than Matthew's allegorical interpretation of the parable concerning lapsed members of the Christian Church (Matthew 18.14) or Luke's stress on the joy in heaven over one sinner who repents (Luke 15.7).[29]

9.15 – Thomas *109*   c

The kingdom is like a man who had a treasure
hidden in his field without knowing it.
After he died, he left it to his son.
The son did not know about it,
accepted it and sold it.
He who bought it found the treasure
while he was ploughing,
He began to lend money to whomever he wished.

This is a more complicated version of the parable than that found in Matthew 13.44, perhaps under the influence of a popular folk-tale. There is a parable attributed to Rabbi Simeon ben Jochai about a man who inherited a field. Since he did not realize that it contained anything precious buried among the rubbish, he sold it at a ridiculously low price. To his great annoyance, he discovered his mistake too late – when the purchaser had bought a palace and slaves, with whom he paraded through the market-place.

The key words of the much shorter parable in Matthew 13.44 are 'in his joy'. In *Thomas*, the person who eventually found the treasure showed his joy by lending money to whomever he wished. He was willing to take risks knowing that he had hidden treasure.

In the rabbinic version of the parable, the final owner built a palace and bought many slaves as a result of finding the hidden treasure. Since the lending of money at interest is contrary to the saying of Jesus in *Thomas* 95 (10.22), this element must have been in the story as the compiler of *Thomas* found it in his source. However, the version of the parable in *Thomas* seems less close to the form in which it was probably told by Jesus and so is graded C. Even so, it is difficult to find gnostic conceptions in it, as some have done.[30]

3 Beatitudes

Of the twelve beatitudes on the lips of Jesus (**8.5**), four (9.16–19) are unfamiliar to readers of the New Testament and sound distinctly odd.

9.16 – Thomas 7   D

Happy is the lion which the man will eat
and the lion will become man
and cursed is the man whom the lion will eat
and the lion will become man.

This odd saying is the first of thirteen beatitudes. Apart from the fragment in Oxyrhynchus Papyrus 654 (6.15), it is not found elsewhere and is rather difficult to interpret. It may refer to the medicinal eating of lion's meat, believed in antiquity to possess healing properties.[31] Or the saying may have been composed in an area where lions were hunted for food or where hunters were eaten by lions.[32] In his letter to Christians in Asia Minor, Peter warns them against their adversary the devil who 'prowls around like a roaring lion, seeking someone to devour' (1 Peter 5.8). In 2 Timothy 4.17, Paul speaks about being rescued from the lion's mouth.

In the curse, the lion seems to get the better of the bargain as in the beatitude, but it may be that there is a scribal error due to tiredness. The text might originally have been, '. . . and the man will become lion'. Some have suggested a reference to Christ as 'the lion of the tribe of Judah' (Revelation 5.5), but this seems rather far-fetched.

9.17 – Thomas 18   D

The disciples said to Jesus:
'Tell us how our end will be.'
Jesus said: 'Have you then discovered the beginning
so that you inquire about the end?
For where the beginning is there shall be the end.
Happy is he who will stand at the beginning.
He will know the end
and will not receive a taste of death.'

A similar question is asked by the disciples in Matthew 24.3, Mark 13.4 and Luke 21.7. In *Thomas* Jesus directs the attention of the disciples away from the end to the beginning. If they understand the beginning they shall also understand the end. They must remember that human beings come from and return to dust (Genesis 3.19). Knowing the end and not tasting death are the rewards given to those who stand as solitaries (*Thomas* 16 – 11.11) and take vows of celibacy (*Thomas* 23 – 12.6) like the encratites at Edessa in Syria. Such people understand all about what happens at the end of time. The beatitude in *Thomas* 18 looks like a blessing on people like the encratites at Edessa; it is unlikely to go back to Jesus, therefore.

9.18 – Thomas 19   C

Happy is he who was before he came into being.
If you become my disciples and hear my words
these stones will minister to you;
for you have five trees in paradise
which are unmoved in summer or in winter
and their leaves do not fall.
Whoever knows them will not taste death.

This seems to be a blessing pronounced by Jesus upon himself as the pre-existent one, as in John 8.58, 'Before Abraham was, I am' and in the *Gospel of Philip* 64.10–12 (14.10). For the idea of hearing the words of Jesus see *Thomas* 38 (10.3) and for not tasting death as the reward of so doing see John 8.31 and 52. Jesus refused to command stones to minister to himself by becoming bread (Matthew 4.3). According to Genesis 3.24 and Revelation 2.7; 22.2, 14, 19, there is one tree in the paradise of God, the tree of life, of whose fruit he who conquers will eat.

9.19 – Thomas 49   D

Happy are the solitary and elect
for you shall find the kingdom
because you come from it
and you shall go there again.

This is one of the beatitudes in *Thomas* that is quite unlike anything in the canonical gospels (**8.5**). It is also one of those sayings containing the Greek word *monachos* (**8.16**). Like the beatitude in *Thomas* 18 (9.17), it pronounces a blessing on celibates.

9.20 – Thomas 54   A

Happy are the poor
for yours is the kingdom of heaven.

This is one of five sayings virtually identical with words of Jesus recorded in the canonical gospels:

Happy are the poor in spirit
for theirs is the kingdom of heaven.

(Matthew 5.3)

Happy are you poor
for yours is the kingdom of God.

(Luke 6.20)

In the first part of this beatitude, *Thomas* (as Luke 6.20) omits 'in spirit' found in Matthew 5.3. The pronoun 'you' found in Luke 6.20 is missing both in Matthew and in *Thomas*. Both Luke and *Thomas* have 'yours' in the second part. While some have argued that this shows evidence of a harmonized text drawn from Matthew and Luke,[33] it is also possible to regard *Thomas* 54 as going back to oral tradition independently of the canonical gospels. *Thomas* 54 may preserve very ancient tradition. It could even be the original form of the saying as spoken by Jesus.[34]

9.21 – Thomas 58   c

Happy is the person who has been labouring;
he has found life.

Since the Coptic word for labour has the same ambiguity as in English, this is a blessing either on those who suffer[35] or on those whose hard work has made them weary,[36] as in Matthew 11.28–30 and *Thomas* 90 (11.14). If the reference is to those who suffer, then parallels can be found in James 1.12: 'Happy is the man who endures trial, for when he has stood the test he will receive the crown of life which God has promised to those who love him'; and in 1 Peter 3.14: 'But even if you were to suffer on account of righteousness, you would be happy.' However, the meaning of the verb here may be 'work' rather than 'suffer'. If so, *Thomas* 58 may be stressing that sustenance for life and the true meaning of life can be found through work. The original curse on the ground, according to Genesis 3.17–19, turns out in the end to be a blessing in disguise. It is through work, of which the most basic form is tilling the ground, that human beings find not only food for themselves and their families but also satisfaction in life.

9.22 – Thomas 68   b

Happy are you when you are hated and persecuted.
Where you have been persecuted
they will not find a place.

In this and the following sayings there is a group of beatitudes approximately equivalent to those found in Matthew 5.10 (and 11), 8 and 6. Here the blessing seems to consist in the denial of a place in the kingdom to those who have persecuted the disciples.[37]

9.23 – Thomas 69a A

*Happy are those who have been persecuted
in their hearts;
These are they who have known the Father in truth.*

This sounds like John's phrases about 'knowing the Father' (John 8.19; 17.7) 'in truth' (John 4.23f.; 17.7; 17.19).

9.24 – Thomas 69b A

*Happy are the hungry;
for their stomachs will be filled.*

For *Thomas* and Luke's 'hungry' (Luke 6.21), Matthew 5.6 has hungering and thirsting after righteousness. The usual rendering of Matthew and Luke, 'they will be satisfied', hides the fact that the Greek verb used is one of animals gorging themselves with hay.[38]

9.25 – Thomas 79b A

*Happy are those who have heard the Father's word
and have kept it in truth.*

This beatitude is also found in Luke 11.28 with slight variations. It stresses that discipleship is more important than any human relationship. As in Luke, it was pronounced by Jesus in response to a beatitude on his mother by a woman in the crowd: 'Happy is the womb that bore you and the breasts that nourished you' (Luke 11.27). The mother of Jesus is never named in *Thomas* but she is referred to again in *Thomas* 99 (10.40) and *Thomas* 101 (12.32).

9.26 – Thomas 79c   A

There will be days when you will say:
Happy is the womb which has not conceived
and the breasts which have not suckled.

This is similar to the beatitude on the childless in Luke 23.29. It has been suggested that *Thomas* 79 has been constructed out of two passages in Luke (Luke 21.23 and Luke 23.29), where they express the priority of discipleship over any human relationship; and that, in *Thomas*, they are intended to be read in the light of the compiler's fastidious abhorrence of sex and are in harmony with the gnostic depreciation of the body.[39] This seems to me to be reading far too much of gnosticism into this document. One would not think of interpreting the similar passages in Luke in such a way.

9.27 – Thomas 103   A

Happy is the person who knows
in which part of the night the robbers will come in,
so that he will rise and collect his . . .
and gird up his loins before they come in.

This beatitude is echoed in a longer saying in *Thomas* 21b (9.5) and in the Q parable of the watchful householder (Matthew 24.42–44; Luke 12.39f.). There does not seem any good reason not to regard it as being authentic, though it is impossible to decide whether it was originally a beatitude or a parable. Perhaps it was uttered in both forms by Jesus on different occasions.

CHAPTER TEN

Hidden Sayings of the Kingdom

1 Hidden Sayings of the Living Jesus

According to the preface to the Coptic *Gospel of Thomas*, all the sayings in it are hidden words spoken by the living Jesus and written down by Didymus Judas Thomas. They are hidden, not because of any gnostic significance, but because only those who have faith can fully understand the teaching of Jesus (Matthew 13.11; Mark 4.11; Luke 8.10). It is like treasure hidden in a field (*Thomas* 109 – 9.15). Once discovered, it brings great joy to the finder.

Jesus is the living one because he is alive now and always. These hidden words were not revealed during some post-resurrection teaching session but during the earthly ministry of Jesus since many of them are also recorded in the canonical gospels.[1]

We have already dealt with all the parables (**9.2**) and beatitudes (**9.3**). In later chapters, we shall be considering those sayings which deal specifically with Jesus (chapter 11) and those which have something to tell us about the Christian life in its various aspects (chapter 12). In this chapter, we look at those which speak about seeking and finding hidden things of one kind or another (**10.2** – 10.1–8), about the mystery of human life (**10.3** – 10.9–13), about leaders who mislead and do not let others enter the kingdom (**10.4** – 10.14–16) and about Jesus' attitude to Jewish legalism and acts of piety which can keep people out of the kingdom unless done for the right reasons (**10.5** – 10.17–23).

Finally, in **10.6**, consideration is given to the idea of the kingdom that is central both to the synoptic gospels and to *Thomas*. When will the kingdom come? Is it already here or is there still something to look forward to in the future? The answer given in *Thomas* is found in several sayings, some of which we have already discussed in chapter 9.

Problems have been encountered in our attempt to group the hidden sayings of Jesus according to form (parables and beatitudes) in chapter 9 and thematically in chapters 10 to 12. For one thing, many of the composite sayings contain more than one theme and could be placed in more than one chapter. Again, extracting parables and beatitudes from the general mass and considering them as special types has meant that the teaching of the living Jesus on certain subjects has been dispersed. This is particularly true with regard to what we can learn from *Thomas* about the kingdom of God. It is in an attempt to redress this balance that we consider at the end of this chapter some sayings of Jesus on this subject not already discussed and recall others that have been examined in chapter 9.

2 Seeking and Finding

10.1 – Thomas 1   D

Whoever finds the interpretation of these words will not receive a taste of death.

Elsewhere in *Thomas*, people find the kingdom (*Thomas* 27 – 10.34; *Thomas* 49 – 9.19), Jesus (*Thomas* 38 – 10.3), a pearl (*Thomas* 76 – 9.10), the body (*Thomas* 80 – 10.8), a lost sheep (*Thomas* 107 – 9.14), treasure (*Thomas* 109 – 9.15). Here it is a case of finding the meaning of these hidden sayings or perhaps even of committing them to writing. The Greek word for interpretation can also mean the ability to put ideas into words.[2] This is what Didymus Judas Thomas was asked to do by the living Jesus, according to the preface, and what Mark did when he became the interpreter of Peter and recorded the apostle's memories of Jesus in his gospel.[3]

10.2 – Thomas 2   c

Let him who seeks continue seeking until he finds:
and when he finds, he will become troubled.
When he has become troubled
he will wonder and he will reign over all things.

The ideas of seeking and finding are frequent in *Thomas* and also in the Wisdom literature, where Wisdom is spoken of as a woman. She calls people to follow her (Ecclesiasticus 6.18) and to seek her diligently (Proverbs 8.17). Those who do not do so will not find her (Proverbs 1.28). According to gnosticism, seeking and finding lead on to knowing. The fact that this third stage is omitted suggests that this is not a gnostic document. Instead, there are another three steps – being troubled, wondering and reigning over all things. According to Genesis 1.29, God gave human beings dominion over every living thing that moves upon the earth.[4]

10.3 – Thomas 38   c

Many times have you desired
to hear these words which I say to you
and you have no other from whom to hear them.
There will be days when you will seek me
and you will not find me.

In a Q passage (3.2) found in Matthew 13.17 and Luke 10.24, Jesus declares that many prophets, righteous ones (Matthew) or kings (Luke) longed (Matthew) or desired (Luke) to see what the disciples are seeing and did not and to hear what they are hearing and did not. According to John 6.68, Peter realized that no one else but Jesus had words of eternal life. Jesus warned the Jews that they would look for him and not find him (John 7.34), just as in Proverbs 1.28 Wisdom declared that people would seek diligently for her and not find her.

10.4 – Thomas 92   c

Seek and you will find.
Yet what you asked about in former times
and which I did not tell you then
now I desire to tell
but you do not inquire after it.

In Matthew 7.7 and Luke 11.9 (Q), asking, seeking and knocking are used as metaphors for persistent prayer. Here we have the second of these with a variation of the first as metaphors of searching for the truth. In this enigmatic saying, Jesus seems to be suggesting that the disciples should be continuing to ask him questions about matters concerning which they are now ready to hear the answers. Previously, they were not in such a position.

10.5 – Thomas 94   A

He who seeks will find
and he who knocks will be let in.

After the interruption of *Thomas* 93 (12.28), this saying returns to the theme of seeking and finding that introduces *Thomas* 92 (10.4) and adds the knocking that completes the trilogy found in the saying in Matthew 7.7 and Luke 11.9 (Q).

10.6 – Thomas 110   c

Whoever has found the world and become rich
let him renounce the world.

This is one of several sayings about world renunciation. The Coptic text uses the Greek verb found in Luke 9.23 of denying oneself in order to 'come after' Jesus.[5]

10.7 – Thomas 56 C

***Whoever has known the world has found a corpse
and whoever has found a corpse
of him the world is not worthy.***

The first clause is repeated in *Thomas* 110 (10.6) with slight variations. The second is repeated in *Thomas* 80 (10.8) with 'body' instead of 'corpse'. In Hebrews 11.38, the world is said not to be worthy of the faithful martyrs. Here it is not worthy of those who have discovered its true nature. Such people realize that the world is mortal, subject to decay and death.

10.8 – Thomas 80 C

***Whoever has known the world has found the body
and whoever has found the body,
of him the world is not worthy.***

This is a doublet of *Thomas* 56 (10.7). The same Aramaic word may lie behind both 'body' and 'corpse'.[6]

---

3 The Mystery of Human Life

10.9 – Thomas 67 D

***The person who knows all things
while failing to know himself
has missed everything.***

Self-knowledge is stressed also in *Thomas* 3 (10.24). It is difficult to know what is meant by knowing all things.[7] In 1 Corinthians 13.9, Paul warns us that our knowledge is imperfect. Yet Jesus promised his disciples that the Spirit would lead them into all truth (John 16.13).

10.10 – Thomas 29   D

*If the flesh has come into existence
because of the spirit
it is a wonder;
but if the spirit has come into existence
because of the body
it is a wonder of wonder.
But I am amazed how this great wealth
has made its home in this poverty.*

The spirit of a person is superior to flesh and body, which are
equated here as in 1 Corinthians 15.35–39, where Paul discusses
the body with which the dead are raised and declares that there
are different kinds of flesh. In *Thomas* 29, the clauses beginning
with 'if' state alternatives, both of which are rejected on account
of their improbability. The mystery of the existence of the
material world remains. All that can be done is to wonder in
amazement. The greatest wonder of all is how such great wealth,
that is, the human spirit, has come to live in such poverty, that
is, the frail human body. The mystery of life causes wonder to all
human beings.

10.11 – Thomas 81   C

*Let him who has become rich become king
and let him who has power renounce it.*

Renunciation is required of those who wish to become disciples,
as in Luke 14.33 – 'So therefore everyone of you who does not
say goodbye to all his possessions cannot be my disciple.'

10.12 – Thomas 87   D

*Wretched is the body which depends upon a body
and wretched is the soul
which depends upon these two.*

If this were a genuine saying, it might lend support to vegetarians who refuse to eat meat from animals. Yet the eating of the flesh of lions seems to be encouraged according to *Thomas* 7 (9.16). Nor does the eating of meat seem to be forbidden in *Thomas* 11 (12.5) and *Thomas* 60 (10.33). What is being referred to here, however, is over-dependence upon physical realities and neglect of the spiritual.

10.13 – Thomas *112* D

Woe to the flesh which depends upon the soul.
Woe to the soul which depends upon the flesh.

Here flesh and soul are opposed to each other; but the meaning seems to be the same as in *Thomas* 29 (10.10), where body and flesh are equated in opposition to spirit. So spirit would seem to be equated with soul. The message of *Thomas* 29 (10.10), 87 (10.12) and 112 is similar. The spirit or the soul of a person should be as independent as possible from the physical body which it inhabits.

---

4 Misguided Leaders

10.14 – Thomas 34 A

If a blind man leads a blind man
both of them are
in the habit of falling[8] into a pit.

This is one of five sayings virtually identical with synoptic sayings;[9] it is closer to the form in Matthew 15.14 than to that in Luke 6.39.[10] Paul echoes this saying in Romans 2.19 – 'You are sure that you are a guide of blind people, a light to those in darkness.' Since it is attested in at least two independent sources (Q and *Thomas*), it probably goes back in some form or other to Jesus.

10.15 – Thomas 39   A

*The Pharisees and the scribes have received
the keys of knowledge and have hidden them.
They did not enter
and they did not let those enter who wished;
but you must be wise as serpents
and innocent as doves.*

In Matthew 23.13, scribes and Pharisees are denounced for
neither entering the kingdom themselves nor allowing others to
do so. Luke 11.52 has a reference to the key of knowledge taken
away by lawyers. *Thomas* 39 contains the only occurrence of
gnosis ('knowledge') in *Thomas*, though verbs for knowing are
frequent. The saying about serpents and doves occurs in
Matthew 10.16 within the context of the missionary charge to
the twelve.

10.16 – Thomas 102   B

*Woe to the Pharisees.
They are like a dog sleeping
in the manger of the oxen.
Neither does he eat
nor does he allow the oxen to eat.*

This woe is unlike any of the seven in Matthew 23.1–36 or the
six in Luke 11.42–52, though the meaning is similar to the first
in Matthew and the sixth in Luke, echoed in *Thomas* 39 (10.15).

The dog in the manger was proverbial in early centuries,
though it has not been found in Greek literature prior to the
time of Jesus. Nevertheless, it was told as a fable by Aesop, who
is said to have lived in Egypt in the sixth century BC. Jesus could
well have adapted it in this original and arresting way to describe
the attitude of the Pharisees.

5 Jewish Legalism and Acts of Piety

10.17 – Thomas 6   B

Do not lie and do not do what you hate;
for all things are uncovered before heaven.
For there is nothing hidden
that shall not be revealed
and there is nothing covered
that shall remain without being uncovered.

The disciples had asked Jesus about three typical Jewish acts of piety – fasting, prayer and almsgiving. In Matthew 6.2–6, 16–18, Jesus did not dispute that these were necessary in the religious life. What troubled him was that these right acts were often performed for the wrong reason – to be seen by other people.[11] In *Thomas* Jesus plays down these pious acts – both here and in *Thomas* 14 (10.18). Fasting, on the other hand, seems to be encouraged in *Thomas* 27 (10.34).

At first sight, Jesus seems to ignore the request for help in the performance of these religious acts and insists instead upon right conduct. However, we may have evidence here and in *Thomas* 7 (9.16) and *Thomas* 8 (9.1) of a tired scribe.[12]

The right conduct referred to by Jesus is given here in negative form, 'Do not lie and do not do what you hate', as compared with the positive command in the golden rule of Matthew 7.12: 'All things that you wish people to do to you, so also do to them.'[13] Differences between Matthew 10.26 and *Thomas* 6 may indicate its independence of Matthew or of Matthew's source.[14]

10.18 – Thomas 14   C

If you fast you will beget sin for yourselves;
and if you pray you will be condemned;
and if you give alms you will do evil to your spirit.
And if you go into any land and wander in the regions
if they receive you eat what they set before you,

heal the sick among them.
For what goes into your mouth will not defile you,
but what comes out of your mouth,
that is what will defile you.

This saying contains a strange mixture of various themes. First comes the answer to the questions asked by the disciples in *Thomas* 6 (10.17) – the prohibition of the three pious acts that are taken for granted in Matthew 6.2–6, 16–18 provided they are done for the right reason. This is followed by phrases reminiscent of the charges given to missionaries in Luke 10.8 and 9 and in Matthew 10.8. Finally, the statement about defilement coming from within rather than from without resembles Matthew 15.11 with its double reference to mouth, rather than Mark 7.15.

10.19 – Thomas 44   c

Whoever blasphemes against the Father,
it shall be forgiven him;
and whoever blasphemes against the Son,
it shall be forgiven him;
but whoever blasphemes against the Holy Spirit,
it shall not be forgiven him
either in heaven or on earth.

In the synoptic gospels, Jesus declares that blasphemy against the Son of man will be forgiven but not blasphemy against the Spirit (Matthew 12.31f.; Luke 12.10). Here in Thomas and also in Tatian (**8.13**), blasphemy against the Father will be forgiven as well. In 1 Corinthians 12.3, Paul roundly denounces blasphemy against the Son.

10.20 – Thomas 53   c

His disciples said to him:
'Is circumcision profitable or not?'
He said to them:

> *'If it were profitable,*
> *their fathers would beget them*
> *circumcised from their mother;*
> *but the true circumcision in spirit*
> *has become profitable in every way.'*

Paul asks a similar question in Romans 3.1 and gives a positive answer to it in the following verse. Yet he also maintained that the true circumcision was a matter of the heart, directed by the Spirit and not by written precepts (Romans 2.29). He may have been echoing a saying of Jesus such as this one in *Thomas* 53, which plays down the physical rite of circumcision. The argument used here is exactly the argument used by Tineus Rufus, Roman Governor of Judaea from AD 132, in a debate with Rabbi Akiba, who died in AD 135. Tineus Rufus pointed out that, if circumcision was necessary, children would be born circumcised.[15] Perhaps he had heard this saying from Christians.

10.21 – Thomas 89   B

Why do you wash the outside of the cup?
Do you not understand that he who made the inside
is also he who made the outside?

In Matthew 23.25 and Luke 11.39, the Pharisees are said to cleanse the outside of the cup and of the plate or dish while inside they are full of wickedness.

10.22 – Thomas 95   A

If you have money do not lend at interest
but give to him
from whom you will not receive it back.

There are warnings in the Old Testament to Jews not to lend money at interest to fellow-Jews who are poor (Leviticus 25.35–37) or even to those who are not poor (Deuteronomy 23.19), though they are permitted to lend to foreigners (Deuteronomy 15.6; 23.20; 28.12). In spite of the prohibition of lending to fellow-Jews, one of the accusations made by Nehemiah at the time of the rebuilding of the walls of Jerusalem was, 'You are exacting interest each from his brother' (Nehemiah 5.7). According to one of the psalmists, one of the characteristics of the truly religious person is that he 'does not put out his money at interest' (Psalm 15.5). In Luke 6.35, Jesus tells his disciples to lend, expecting nothing in return. In contrast to this, in the parable of the talents (Matthew 25.27) and the parable of the pounds (Luke 19.23), there is clear instruction about investing money at the bank so that the owner might receive his own back with interest.

10.23 – Thomas 104   c

**Which sin have I committed
or in what have I been vanquished?
But when the bridegroom
comes out of the bridal chamber
then let them fast and let them pray.**

A similar reply was given to his family when they invited Jesus to accompany him to be baptized by John the Baptist, according to the *Gospel of the Nazaraeans* (15.1). Here the disciples had suggested that they should pray and fast on a particular day. The time would come when these pious acts would be appropriate, when the bridegroom had left them (Mark 2.19; Matthew 9.15; Luke 5.34).

6 When will the kingdom come?

The Coptic word for 'kingdom' occurs twenty times in *Thomas*, though the phrase 'kingdom of God', so common in the synoptic gospels (Matthew, Mark and Luke), never appears. Instead, the word 'kingdom' is found on its own twelve times. In addition, 'the kingdom of the Father' occurs six times, 'the kingdom of my

Father' once and 'the kingdom of heaven' (found over thirty times in Matthew) occurs once.

As in the synoptic gospels, many of these sayings in *Thomas* stress the present reality of the kingdom. Jesus claimed that the kingdom or reign of God had already dawned with his coming. This is what is known as realized eschatology – the end (*eschaton*) for which the Jews were looking had come and the Messiah had arrived. However, there are also sayings in the synoptic gospels that look forward to a fuller coming in the future, either in this world or the next. So the term realized eschatology has been modified to inaugurated eschatology.[16]

It is sometimes claimed that in *Thomas* only the element of realized eschatology is present and that the idea of future fulfilment is lacking. As Robert Grant put it, 'He has made the kingdom almost exclusively present, while in our gospels it is partly present but will be fully realized only in the future. Such a doctrine is essentially gnostic, not Christian.'[17]

It is true that, in many sayings in *Thomas*, stress is laid on the present reality of the kingdom. It is already the possession of the poor, who are declared to be happy (*Thomas* 54 – 9.20). Other beatitudes stress the present blessedness of 'the solitary and elect' (*Thomas* 49 – 9.19), those who work or suffer (*Thomas* 58 – 9.21), the hated and persecuted (*Thomas* 68 – 9.22), the hungry (*Thomas* 69b – 9.24), those who have heard the Father's word (*Thomas* 79b – 9.25) and the watchful householder (*Thomas* 103 – 9.27).

When we were examining parables, also in chapter 9, we saw how the discovery of the kingdom can bring great joy, as when a fisherman catches a large fish (*Thomas* 8 – 9.1) or when a farmer finds hidden treasure while ploughing a field he has just bought (*Thomas* 109 – 9.15). The kingdom is enduring treasure, whose value can be compared to that of a precious pearl bought by a merchant for the price of all his merchandise (*Thomas* 76 – 9.10). In the parable of the sower and the soils, some of the seed sown has fallen upon good soil and a harvest has already been reaped (*Thomas* 9 – 9.2).

The presence of the kingdom is also implied in sayings about the kingdom within one (*Thomas* 3 – 10.24); 'what you expect', 'rest' (of the dead) and 'the new world' (*Thomas* 51 – 10.29);

'becoming as a child' and 'knowing the kingdom' (*Thomas* 46 – 12.3). In all of these the kingdom is already present with the coming of Jesus.

However, there are many sayings in which the reference is definitely to the future. The growth of the kingdom is likened to that of a mustard seed which produces large branches as shelter for birds (*Thomas* 20 – 9.3) and that of large loaves from a lump of dough as the result of a little leaven (*Thomas* 96 – 9.11). Warnings about being prepared for death are found in the parables of the children undressing in a field (*Thomas* 21a – 9.4) and of the rich man who filled his storehouses with fruit (*Thomas* 63 – 9.7). As a householder stays awake to protect his house from a thief (*Thomas* 21b – 9.5) and receives congratulations for his watchfulness (*Thomas* 103 – 9.27), so disciples are to exercise watchfulness for the day of judgement. This event will be like the harvest. Wheat will be separated from the weeds that are destined for destruction (*Thomas* 57 – 9.6).

In addition, there are sayings in which an equivalent word or phrase is used instead of 'kingdom'; for example, 'the place of life' (*Thomas* 4 – 10.27), 'the end' (*Thomas* 18 – 9.17), 'the places of my Father' (*Thomas* 64 – 9.8), 'a place of rest' (*Thomas* 60 – 10.33). Overconfidence in one's ability to reach the kingdom in one's own strength is discouraged in the cautionary tale about the woman carrying a jar of meal found empty when she arrived home (*Thomas* 97 – 9.12). The kingdom is the final destiny of the solitary and elect, as it was also their origin (*Thomas* 49 – 9.19); *Thomas* 50 – 12.24).

In all of these sayings, Jesus is referring to something in the future, whether it be to the further growth of the kingdom or to the death of the Christian or to the day of judgement. Even though canonical sayings about the future coming of the Son of man are absent from *Thomas*,[18] there is an 'end' (*eschaton*) that has still to come (*Thomas* 18 – 9.17). On that day, messengers (or angels) and prophets will 'give you what is yours and take what is theirs' (*Thomas* 88 – 10.39). The eschatology of *Thomas* is not all realized, any more than it is in the New Testament. In what follows, the present reality of the kingdom is implied in 10.24 to 10.31. There is a future reference in 10.29 to 10.40.

10.24 – Thomas 3   c

If those who lead you say to you:
'See, the kingdom is in heaven';
then the birds of heaven will precede you.
If they say to you: 'It is in the sea';
then the fish will precede you.
But the kingdom is within you and it is outside you.
When you know yourselves
then you will be known
and you will know that you are
the sons of the living Father.
But if you do not know yourselves
then you are really poor.

Leaders who mislead are blind guides in Matthew 15.14; 23.16; Luke 6.39; *Thomas* 34 (10.14). The kingdom is not in heaven nor in the sea (Deuteronomy 30.11–14; *Baruch* 3.29f.; Romans 10.6f.) but within you. Up to this point, *Thomas* 3 seems to be an expansion of the saying found in Luke 17.20f. in the light of Deuteronomy 30.11–14. However, while Luke 17.21 should probably be translated as 'the kingdom of God is amongst you', in Oxyrhynchus Papyrus 654 (6.11) and *Thomas* 3 it is quite clear that the kingdom is within you. The nearness of the kingdom is stressed also in *Thomas* 51 (10.29) and *Thomas* 113 (10.28). The self-knowledge stressed in the second part of the saying is that of those who have been baptized and know that they are children of God.

10.25 – Thomas 22a   A

These children being suckled
are like those who enter the kingdom.

The condition for entering the kingdom is the willingness to receive something for nothing – the grace of God that we have done nothing to deserve. We have to be 'born again' (John 3.3) and 'become as children' (Matthew 18.3), for to such the kingdom belongs (Mark 10.14; Luke 18.16).

10.26 – Thomas 22b D

**When you make the two one
and when you make the inner as the outer
and the outer as the inner
and the above as the below;
and when you make the male and female
into a single one
so that the male will not be male
and the female not be female;
when you make the eyes in place of an eye
and a hand in the place of a hand
and a foot in the place of a foot
and an image in place of an image;
then you shall enter the kingdom.**

The disciples accept Jesus' equation of becoming as a child with entering the kingdom (*Thomas* 22a – 10.25) by asking: 'Shall we then as children enter the kingdom?' In reply, Jesus adds a third equivalent, achieving a state of asexuality. On its own, the phrase 'make the two one' could simply reflect the 'one flesh' of Genesis 2.24; but phrases that follow make it clear that the reference is to the rejection of sexuality. This would be in line with the encratism of the early Syrian Church (**8.14**), where the saying may have been composed.

10.27 – Thomas 4 c

**The old man will not hesitate to ask
a little child of seven days
about the place of life
and he will live.
For many who are first will become last
and they will become a single one.**

In the parallel in Oxyrhynchus Papyrus 654 (6.12), some words and lines are missing. In Matthew 11.25 and Luke 10.21 (Q), Jesus thanks God for his revelation of the truth to babes rather than to the wise and understanding. The place of life is the place of final destiny, as in *Thomas* 24 (12.11); *Thomas* 60 (10.33); *Thomas* 64 (9.8); *Thomas* 68 (9.22); Luke 16.28; John 14.2. The saying about first becoming last is often on the lips of Jesus. Its sequel, 'and the last first', found, for example, in Mark 10.31 and Oxyrhynchus Papyrus 654 (6.12), has been omitted here, though it seems to be necessary in order to make sense of the following words. Like eternal life, a constant theme in the Fourth Gospel, becoming a single one (*Thomas* 23 – 12.6; *Thomas* 49 – 9.19) is also something that can happen in the present life (**8.16**). The phrase was used as a description of the celibate life of encratites (**8.14**) in the early Syrian Church in and around Edessa. While this part of the composite saying seems to have been influenced by its place of origin, the rest could possibly go back to Jesus (C).

10.28 – Thomas *113*   A

His disciples said to him:
'When will the kingdom come?'
Jesus said:
'It will not come by expectation.
They will not say:
"See, here" or "See, there".
But the kingdom of the Father
is spread upon the earth
and people do not see it.'

There are many sayings in the canonical gospels in which Jesus declares that the kingdom of God is already present in his own ministry. In the parable of the seed growing secretly (Mark 4.26–29), its invisibility is stressed, as here.

10.29 – Thomas 51 c

**What you expect has come
but you know it not.**

The disciples want to know when the rest of the dead and the
new world will come. Jesus replies that the future is already
present, as he does also with regard to the kingdom in *Thomas*
113 (10.28). Christians are living in the new world, even though
they may not realize it. 'Rest' is the catchword linking this saying
with the previous one. It is a synonym for salvation.[19]

10.30 – Thomas 59 A

**Look upon the living one
as long as you live
so that you may not die
and seek to see him
and be unable to see him.**

Jesus himself is referred to as the living one in *Thomas* 52 (11.3).
He speaks words of eternal life (John 6.68) and those who
believe in him shall never die (John 11.26). In John 7.34, Jesus
warns the Jews that the time would come when they would seek
him and not find him.

10.31 – Thomas 70 c

**When you bring forth him
whom you have within you
he will save you.
If you do not have him within you
he will kill you.**

This may be a reference to the Holy Spirit, without whose help
no one can really live. In Romans 8.9–11, Paul speaks about the
Spirit of God and also about the risen Christ dwelling in
Christians. Similarly, in the parable of the vine Jesus speaks

about the mutual indwelling of Christ and his disciples – 'Remain in me and I in you. As the branch cannot bear fruit by itself, unless it remains on the vine, neither can you unless you remain in me' (John 15.4).

10.32 – Thomas 5 B

Know what is in front of you
and what is hidden from you
will be uncovered to you.
For there is nothing hidden
which will not be revealed.

To what was Jesus referring in this saying about hidden things being revealed? Was it his own preaching, as in Mark 4.22 and Luke 8.17, or was it the fearless preaching of the disciples, as in Matthew 10.26 and possibly Luke 12.2 and 3 (Q), or was it the hypocrisy of the Pharisees, as in Luke 12.1? Perhaps the synoptic evangelists no longer knew the original meaning of the saying of Jesus, to which *Thomas* may be pointing.[20] When all things come to an end, everything will be revealed and our knowledge will be complete, as Paul suggests in 1 Corinthians 13.12. This early form of the saying is also reflected in 1 Corinthians 4.5, where Paul speaks of the time when the Lord will bring to light the things now hidden in darkness. In the meantime, we can know what lies in front of us, Jesus himself, whom disciples can know right now and who can reveal to them things that are hidden from other people (Mark 4.11). Oxyrhynchus Papyrus 654 (6.13) has an additional phrase – 'and buried that will not be raised up' – absent also from the synoptic versions.

10.33 – Thomas 60 D

Jesus said to his disciples:
'Why does this man carry the lamb with him?'
The disciples said to him:
'In order that he may kill it and eat it.'

He said to them:
'As long as it is alive he will not eat it;
but only if he has killed it
and it has become a corpse.'
They said:
'Otherwise he will not be able to do it.'
He said to them:
'You yourselves seek a place of rest for yourselves
lest you become a corpse and be eaten up.'

In this narrative, one of only a few in *Thomas* (8.2), the sight of a man carrying a lamb on its way to slaughter is used as a warning to the disciples not to be worried about their own ultimate destiny since that is already assured. In John 14.1–6, Jesus declares that he is going to prepare a place for his disciples so that they may be with him. In Hebrews 4.11, we are urged to strive to enter the rest prepared by God for his people.

10.34 – Thomas 27 c

If you do not fast from the world
you will not find the kingdom;
if you keep not the sabbath as sabbath,
you will not see the Father.

The first half of this saying, found also in Oxyrhynchus Papyrus 1 (6.2), seems to contradict the first part of *Thomas* 14 (10.18); but it is more in accord with Matthew 6.16–18, where Jesus does not condemn fasting as such but demands that the motive should be pure. Here Jesus sees fasting as a condition of finding the kingdom. In Matthew 6.33 and Luke 12.31, disciples are encouraged to seek first his (the Father's) kingdom. Jesus proceeds to uphold another Jewish religious observance, keeping the sabbath. As with almsgiving, praying and fasting in Matthew 6.2–6, 16–18, it is the right performance that is insisted upon.

10.35 – Thomas 61   c

'Two will rest on a bed:
the one will die, the other will live.'
Salome said:
'Who are you, man, and whose son are you?
You took your seat upon my bench
and ate from my table.'
Jesus said to her:
'I am he who is from one who is equal;
to me was given the things of my Father.'
Salome said:
'I am your disciple.'
Jesus said to her:
'Therefore I say, if he is the same,
he will be filled with light;
but if he is divided,
he will be filled with darkness.'

The first saying, similar to that in Luke 17.34, stresses the universality of judgement, its unexpected arrival and the fact that it will not respect family ties.

Salome, one of the women disciples of Jesus who later saw him being crucified and visited the tomb on Easter Day (Mark 15.40; 16.1), thought she should know who Jesus was because she had given him hospitality. Yet she was puzzled by him, as were the Pharisees on account of the people with whom he had table fellowship (Matthew 9.11; Mark 2.16; Luke 5.30). Jesus explains to her his divine origin in terms reminiscent of the statements in the Fourth Gospel of the equality and subordination in the relationship between the Son and the Father (John 3.35; 5.18; 10.18, 30; 13.3). Jesus' explanation in terms of his divine origin seems to satisfy Salome and to quell her doubts about allowing Jesus to sit at her table. Perhaps it was a matter of social etiquette that a man should not accept hospitality from a single woman, or even from a married woman if her husband was not present.

The rather obscure saying with which *Thomas* 61 ends seems to contain echoes of statements about the Word, which was the

same as God, being also the true light that enlightens every man
(John 1.1, 9).

10.36 – Thomas 83   D

*The images are visible to men
but the light within them is hidden.
In the image of the light of the Father
the light of the images will be revealed.
His image is concealed by his light.*

This and the following three sayings depend on themes found in
the first two chapters of Genesis. Yet the word 'image' is used in
two senses. In the plural, it signifies material things seen by men
and women though their real meaning is hidden from them.
Only God can reveal this to them though he himself cannot be
seen by human beings (Exodus 33.20; Job 19.26; John 1.28). The
image of the light of the Father could be Jesus, 'the image of the
invisible God' (Colossians 1.15). For the close association of
'image' and 'light', compare *Thomas* 50 (12.24).

10.37 – Thomas 84   D

*When you see your likeness you rejoice.
But when you see your images
which came into being before you
and which neither die nor become visible
how much you will have to bear!*

A distinction is made here between the image in which man was
created by God and his likeness (Genesis 1.26). While we are
here on earth, we see only a likeness as in a mirror (1
Corinthians 13.12) but hereafter we shall see face to face the
image according to which men and women were created. Then
we shall discover how far short we really have been of the glory
of God for which we were made.

10.38 – Thomas 85   D

Adam came into existence
from a great power and a great wealth
and yet he did not become worthy of you.
For if he had been worthy
he would not have experienced death.

In spite of Adam's great privileges of power and wealth, he sinned by disobeying the known will of God and so became unworthy. Death is regarded as the punishment for Adam's sin.

10.39 – Thomas 88   D

Messengers and prophets will come to you
and give you what is yours.
You will give them what you have and say:
'When will they come and take what is theirs?'

In Matthew 13.41, it is said that the Son of man will send his messengers (Greek word *angeloi* usually translated 'angels') who will gather out of his kingdom all causes of offences and criminals and throw them into the furnace. Presumably *Thomas* 88 also refers to the last judgement, when both those who have done good and those who have done evil will be rewarded appropriately.

10.40 – Thomas 99   A

Those here who do the will of my Father
are my brothers and my mother.
These are they who will enter
the kingdom of my Father.

To a slight variation of the saying found in Matthew 12.49f.; Mark 3.34f.; Luke 8.21 has been added the second sentence, showing that *Thomas* is independent of the canonical gospels.

The character of the spiritual family being hinted at here is made clearer in *Thomas* 101 (12.32).

10.41 – Thomas *111* c

The heavens and the earth will be rolled up
in your presence.
Whoever lives on the living one
will not see death.
The world is not worthy of
the person who finds himself.

In Revelation 6.14, the sky is said to vanish like a scroll that is rolled up. The woman of Samaria at Jacob's well was told that anyone who drank of the water given by Jesus would have a spring of water welling up to eternal life (John 4.14). Of such a person, the world is not worthy for he has discovered that the world is a dead thing, as suggested in *Thomas* 56 (10.7).

CHAPTER ELEVEN

Who is Jesus?

1 In this chapter, we shall consider sayings in the Coptic *Gospel of Thomas* which deal with the person of Jesus (**11.2** – 11.1–8), the purpose of his coming into this world (**11.3** – 11.9–15) and the continual presence of the risen Christ with his followers throughout the centuries (**11.4** – 11.16, 17).

2 The Person of Jesus

11.1 – Thomas 43   B

From what I say, you do not know who I am.
You have become as the Jews;
for they love the tree but hate its fruit.
They love the fruit but hate the tree.

Impressed by the authority of his teaching, the disciples had asked Jesus: 'Who are you that you should say these things to us?' In the synoptic gospels, it is the Jewish leaders who questioned his authority for doing what he did (Matthew 21.23; Mark 11.28; Luke 20.2). According to John 8.25, the Jews as a whole were baffled by his teaching. The disciples should have known better. Good fruit such as Jesus was producing could only come from a good tree. In *Thomas 13* (12.2), on the other hand, Thomas is rebuked by Jesus for calling him Master.

11.2 – Thomas 91   A

*You test the face of the sky and of the earth
and him who is before you you have not known.
You do not know how to test this moment.*

This is another response of Jesus to a question from the disciples as to who he was, this time in order that they might believe in him. In Luke 12.54–56 it is the people, and in Matthew 16.2–3 it is the Pharisees and Sadducees, whom Jesus accuses of not being able to interpret the present time. Here it is the disciples who are unable to discern the significance of Jesus' coming.

11.3 – Thomas 52   B

*You have dismissed the living one
who is before you
and you have spoken about the dead.*

In this response to a statement made by the disciples that twenty-four prophets had spoken about him, Jesus appears to be rebuking the disciples for refusing to accept the one to whom the prophets bore witness. They were turning back to the past when they should be looking upon the living one (*Thomas* 59 – 10.30) who was in their midst. As in the preface, Jesus is the living one because he is alive now and always, as God is the living Father in *Thomas* 50 (12.24). In *Thomas* 37 (12.7), Jesus is the Son of the living one, while in *Thomas* 3 (10.24) the disciples are sons of the living Father.

11.4 – Thomas 15   C

*When you see him who was not born of woman
prostrate yourselves upon your face and worship him.
He is your Father.*

Jesus seems to be referring to himself as being different from ordinary human beings and as being equal to the Father, as in

John 14.9 he declared that anyone who had seen him had seen the Father.

11.5 – Thomas 105   c

Whoever knows father and mother
will be called the son of a harlot.

While this saying may refer to disciples in general, Jesus may be alluding to his divine sonship and his human birth of the Virgin Mary. The insinuation of an illegitimate birth is found several times in Jewish literature.[1]

11.6 – Thomas 31   A

No prophet is acceptable in his village:
no doctor heals those who know him.

This double saying is also amongst the Oxyrhynchus fragments (6.6). There is a parallel to the first part of it in the canonical gospels (Matthew 13.57; Mark 6.4; Luke 4.24; John 4.44). The double saying with its parallel clauses and the reference to a doctor as well as to a prophet could well be authentic and more primitive.[2] It would in fact fit into the context in the synoptic gospels very well. Jesus has been teaching in the synagogue at Nazareth to the great astonishment of all who hear him. According to Mark and Luke, this took place on a sabbath. Matthew omits this detail. The people marvel at the wisdom of his words and at the miraculous power of his hands, at least in other places. Luke omits the reference to the miracles at this point (Luke 4.22), but he is the only one of the four evengelists to quote the proverb about the physician: 'Doctor, heal yourself' (Luke 4.23) – a proverb that seems to be echoed by the Jewish rulers standing at the cross: 'He saved others; he cannot save himself' (Matthew 27.42; Mark 15.31; Luke 23.35).

Several parallels to this proverb have been found. In Book Eleven of Homer's *Iliad*, there is a reference to two surgeons, one of whom was lying wounded in camp in need of a good physician himself. This is the first example in a long line of references to a medical doctor who is himself in need of healing. Euripides speaks of someone who is a doctor of others himself swelling with ulcers (*Frogs* 1071). There is an Arabic proverb about a doctor who cures other people and is himself ill. There is also a Jewish proverb: 'Doctor, heal your own limp.'[3]

11.7 – Thomas 66 A

Show me the stone which the builders rejected.
It is the corner-stone.

This metaphor from building found in Psalm 118.22 is also quoted in Matthew 21.42; Mark 12.10; and Luke 20.17, at the conclusion of the parable of the tenants, with which it is fused. Here it is a separate and isolated saying introduced without any specific reference to the fact that Jesus is appealing to the Old Testament. This may point to the fact that originally it was independent of the parable.

11.8 – Thomas 86 A

The foxes have their holes
and the birds their nest;
but the Son of man has no place
to lay his head and rest.

This is the only 'Son of man' saying in *Thomas*. It is almost exactly the same as the saying found in Matthew 8.20 and Luke 9.58 but there is a significant addition at the very end – 'and rest'. This is not necessarily a gnostic touch.[4] The idea of rest is found both in the Old Testament and in the New Testament. The Hebrew words behind the 'green pastures' of Psalm 23.2 mean 'beside waters of rest'. In Psalm 55.6, the psalmist wishes for wings like a dove in order to fly away and be at rest. The promise of rest is given by Jesus in Matthew 11.28 and *Thomas* 90 (11.14).

3 The Purpose of the Coming of Jesus

11.9 – Thomas 28 c

I stood in the midst of the world
and in human form I appeared to them.
I found them all drunk
and none among them thirsty.
My soul was troubled for the sons of men
because they are blind in their heart.
They do not see that empty
they have come into the world
and empty they seek to go out of the world again.
But now they are drunk.
When they have shaken off their wine,
then they will repent.

In John 1.14, we are told that the Word became a human being and lived among us; but the closest parallel to the first two clauses is found as the first line of an early Christian hymn – 'He appeared in flesh' (1 Timothy 3.16). Just as no one was prepared to listen to Wisdom crying aloud in the street (Proverbs 1.20–24), so Jesus found everyone so filled with ordinary drink that they were not thirsty for the water that he could give to them (John 4.14).

11.10 – Thomas 10 a

I have cast fire upon the world,
and see, I am guarding it until it is ablaze.

In Luke 12.49, the fire is not yet kindled. Here, the process seems to be one stage further on. The fire has been kindled by Jesus but he is keeping guard over it until it is blazing.

11.11 – Thomas 16 B

People may think I have come
to throw peace upon the world
and they do not know that I have come
to throw divisions upon the earth, fire, sword, war.
For there shall be five in a house:
three shall be against two and two against three,
the father against the son
and the son against the father,
and they will stand as solitaries.

To the 'sword' mentioned in Matthew 10.34 (but not in Luke 12.51), *Thomas* has added 'fire' and 'war'. The five people involved are the father and the mother on the one hand and the son, the daughter and the daughter-in-law on the other, though *Thomas* mentions specifically only the father and the son. In any case, it seems to be a case of the generation gap. Although other sayings also in *Thomas* (*Thomas* 55 – 12.31; *Thomas* 79c – 9.26) point to the rejection of the natural family in the interests of higher values, *Thomas* stresses the central place of the family properly understood, as in *Thomas* 101 (12.32). The last clause looks like an addition to the original saying as found in the synoptic gospels by those with extreme ascetic views. Standing as solitaries (**8.16**; *Thomas* 75 – 12.8) or as single ones (**8.17**; *Thomas* 23 – 12.6) seems to be a special term used in the context of vows of celibacy.

11.12 – Thomas 72 A

O man, who made me a divider?
I am not a divider, am I?

This rejoinder to a man who asked Jesus to act as judge in a family dispute about an inheritance is clearly a parallel version of the incident found in Luke 12.13f., where it is followed by the parable of the rich farmer (Luke 12.16–21). In Thomas, Jesus turns to his disciples for corroboration with a question expecting the answer, 'No'. The parable has already been related in *Thomas* 63 (9.7).

11.13 – Thomas 71 A

**I shall destroy this house
and no one will be able to build it again.**

In John 2.19, the reference is to 'this temple', by which Jesus meant the temple of his body (John 2.20). In *Thomas*, the intent may be to indicate the overthrow of the old Jewish regime by Jesus.[5]

11.14 – Thomas 90 A

**Come to me,
for easy is my yoke and my lordship is gentle
and you will find rest for yourselves.**

This is an abridged and emended form of the saying found in Matthew 11.28–30. The invitation of Jesus is similar to that put into the mouth of Wisdom in the Book of Ecclesiasticus 51.23–26, where study of the law is commended. Instead of the yoke of the law, Jesus offers a yoke that is easy. It is possible that this shorter version of the saying is more primitive than that found in Matthew.[6]

11.15 – Thomas 17 C

**I shall give you what eye has not seen
and ear has not heard and hand has not touched
and has not arisen in the human heart.**

In 1 Corinthians 2.9, Paul claims to be quoting from Scripture when he declares that God has revealed 'what eye did not see and ear did not hear and did not enter heart of man'. These phrases echo, but are not identical with, Isaiah 64.4 and 65.17. In *Thomas* 17, the words are found on the lips of Jesus with the addition of 'what hand has not touched'. In Matthew 13.16 and Luke 10.23, Jesus pronounces a beatitude upon those who see and hear him. *Thomas* 17 could be a genuine saying in which Jesus, using familiar words from Scripture, declares that he will give his disciples what has previously been unseen, unheard, untouched and even unimagined.[7]

---

4 The Presence of Jesus

11.16 – Thomas *30* A

Where there are three godly ones,
they are in God;
where there are two or one,
I am with him.

This saying, along with *Thomas* 77 (11.17), contains one of the most important variants between *Thomas* and the Oxyrhynchus papyri fragments. The two sayings are found together in Oxyrhynchus Papyrus 1 (6.5).

The first part of *Thomas* 30 is usually translated:

Where there are three gods
they are gods.

This seems to be teaching that there are three gods, not just one. Yet elsewhere Thomas clearly accepts the fact that there is only one God. For this reason, it has been suggested that the Coptic text must be corrupt at this point. However, it is possible that the solution may lie in an alternative translation, like mine.[8]

In the Jewish *Mishnah*, composed in the second century AD from earlier material, it is said that if the words of the law are spoken between two people sitting together, the divine presence rests between them. Here in *Thomas* 30, in what looks like an expanded version of Matthew 18.20, Jesus promises divine fellowship not only for the minimum number of a gathering together of Christians for worship (two or three) but the realization of the presence of the living Christ by a single

121

disciple. In Matthew 28.20, there is a similar promise to all disciples – 'I am with you always'.

11.17 – Thomas 77 A

I am the light that is above them all.
I am all things:
all things came forth from me
and all things attained to me.
Split a piece of wood, I am there;
lift up the stone and you will find me there.

Jesus is the light of the world (John 8.12), the true light that enlightens every person (John 1.9). It is also 'from him and through him and to him' that all things[9] exist (Romans 11.36) or attain, the Coptic word for which can also mean 'break' or 'split'. This acts as a catchword joining together the two parts of this composite saying. The second part occurs in Oxyrhynchus Papyrus 1 (6.5), but in reverse order. In both places, it is stressed that the presence of the living Christ can transform the daily round and common task into divine service. For the Christian, work is not mere drudgery but an opportunity to deny oneself, a road to bring us daily nearer God.[10]

CHAPTER TWELVE

Who is the Greatest?

1 The Christian Community

A large number of the sayings in the Coptic *Gospel of Thomas* have to do with the Christian community and with discipleship in one form or another. Three of the apostles are specifically named, Peter, Matthew and Thomas, as well as James, the brother of Jesus (**12.2** – 12.1, 2). Thomas is singled out for a private revelation in addition to being given the task of writing down all these hidden words (12.2). John the Baptist is praised (**12.3** – 12.3, 4).

The asceticism that is undoubtedly present in certain passages within the New Testament was taken to extremes in the early Syrian Christian community, where only celibates could be baptized and become full members (**8.14**). This extreme asceticism, known as encratism, shines through in various sayings concerning the solitary and the single ones – sayings which would appear to have been influenced by the Christian community at Edessa and which are probably not to be regarded as going back in their entirety to the teaching of Jesus (**12.4** – 12.5–10). The Coptic phrase 'single one' (**8.17**) is the equivalent of the Greek word *monachos* meaning 'solitary one', from which we get the English word 'monk' (**8.16**).

The characteristics and duties of the Christian life are described in sayings recalling the teaching of Jesus in the New Testament, in particular, the Sermon on the Mount (**12.5** – 12.11–30). Finally, three sayings which warn about the cost of discipleship are grouped together at the end of this chapter (**12.6** – 12.31–33).

---

2 James, Peter, Matthew and Thomas

12.1 – Thomas *12* c

Wherever you are
you will go to James the Just
for whose sake heaven and earth came into being.

In response to a question from the disciples as to who should be their leader after his departure, Jesus nominates his brother, James. The primacy of James is characteristic of Jewish Christianity. According to the *Gospel of the Hebrews* (**15.4**), James the Just was the first person to whom Jesus appeared after his resurrection (15.14). In the New Testament, he is the leader of the Christians in Jerusalem (Acts 15.13; 21.18) and of the Jewish party in the early Church (Galatians 1.19; 2.9, 12).

12.2 – Thomas *13* d

I am not your Master
because you drank and became drunk
from the bubbling stream which I have measured out.

When Jesus asked his disciples whom he was like, Peter likened him to a righteous messenger (or angel), Matthew compared him with a wise philosopher, but Thomas, addressing Jesus as 'Master', declared that he was unable to make any comparison in human terms. This was Jesus' response to Thomas, in the first instance a rebuke for calling Jesus his Master. As a disciple, he is not a slave but a friend (John 15.15). Then Jesus took Thomas aside and spoke three words to him, which Thomas refused to reveal to the others. This may be a reference to John 14.6, where we are told it was to Thomas that Jesus declared that he was the way and the truth and the life. In *Thomas* 13, Thomas has the role assigned to Peter in the synoptic account of the incident at

Caesarea Philippi. He is the one to whom the revelation has been given, not by the Father, as in Matthew 16.17, but by Jesus, who has provided him with the bubbling spring like the spring of living water welling up to eternal life in John 4.14.

---

3 John the Baptist

12.3 – Thomas 46 B

From Adam until John the Baptist
there is among those born of women
none greater than John the Baptist
so that his eyes will not be broken;
but I have said that
whoever among you becomes as a child
shall know the kingdom
and he shall become greater than John.

This is similar to the saying about John the Baptist in Matthew 11.11 and Luke 7.28 (Q) with the addition of what looks like his reward for faithful witness to Jesus. He will not experience the full bitterness of death (literally, 'his eyes will not be broken').[1] Yet any Christian is greater than John (Matthew 11.11; Luke 7.28) and can know the kingdom by receiving it as a child (*Thomas* 22a – 10.25).

12.4 – Thomas 78 A

Why did you come out into the desert?
To see a reed shaken by the wind?
And to see a man clothed in soft garments?
Kings and your great ones
are those clothed in fine garments
and they are unable to discern the truth.

In Matthew 11.7 and Luke 7.24 (Q), similar words are addressed to the crowds concerning John the Baptist, who is not named here in *Thomas*.

---

4 The Solitary and Single Ones

12.5 – Thomas 11   D

This heaven shall pass away
and the one above it shall pass away
and the dead are not alive
and the living shall not die.
In the days when you devoured the dead
you made it alive.
When you come into the light what will you do?
On the day when you were one you became two.
But when you have become two what will you do?

This is a difficult saying which seems to have been made up from different sources. It opens with words found in the synoptic gospels (Matthew 24.35; Mark 13.31; Luke 21.33). Then comes the metaphor of the living eating the dead and thereby endowing it with life, which recalls the beatitude on the lion in *Thomas* 7 (9.16). The reference to light is reminiscent of John, where light is a constant theme. Finally, the one becoming two seems to contradict the ideas found elsewhere in *Thomas* of becoming a single one and of the solitary one obtaining salvation.

12.6 – Thomas 23   D

I shall choose you one out of a thousand
and two out of ten thousand
and they shall stand as a single one.

The choice of the disciples by Jesus in the past (John 6.70; 13.18; 15.16; 15.19) is here transferred to the future and is linked to the call to celibacy (**8.17**), a characteristic of the early Syrian Church.

12.7 – Thomas 37   D

When you take off your clothes
without being ashamed
and take your clothes
and put them under your feet
and tread on them
then you shall see the Son of the living one
and you shall not fear.

This strange saying reminds one of the parable of the children in the field (*Thomas* 21a – 9.4), where death is compared with undressing. Here the words attributed to Jesus are given as the response to a question as to when Jesus will be revealed to the disciples. At first sight, it seems to envisage a return to the innocence of Adam and Eve before the fall (Genesis 2.25; 3.7). The reference to treading on one's clothes, however, suggests that the imagery may be that of undressing as a preliminary to Christian baptism (Ephesians 4.22; Colossians 3.9) rather than the rejection of sexuality.[2] Both ideas were found together in the Syrian Church in the first centuries, since baptism was confined to celibates. This could be another link in the chain connecting this document with Edessa (**8.14**). Clement of Alexandria quotes a similar saying from the *Gospel of the Egyptians* (15.15).

12.8 – Thomas 75   D

Many are standing at the door
but the solitary are the ones
who will enter the bridal chamber.

In Matthew 22.14, many are called but few are chosen. In the parable of the ten bridesmaids (Matthew 25.1–13), those who were ready went in to the marriage feast with the bridegroom. The bridal chamber occurs again in *Thomas* 104 (10.23), though there it is a case of the bridegroom coming out of it rather than of others entering it. *Thomas* 75 reflects the situation in the early Church in eastern Syria, where only celibates could be baptized and become full members. Others could only 'stand at the door' as adherents (**8.14**). The refrain in one of Ephraem's 'Hymns on Virginity' runs: 'Make me, too, worthy to enter into the bridechamber of your glory, clothed in your raiment, Lord.'[3]

12.9 – Thomas 106   D

**When you make the two one
you will become sons of man,
and when you say,
'Mountain, be moved',
it will be moved.**

This is a developed form of a saying found in *Thomas* 48 (12.23). Here, the union of opposites is being hinted at – the union of male and female, inner and outer, above and below – as seen in *Thomas* 22b (10.26). Unity takes the place here of faith as the force that removes mountains (Matthew 17.20; 21.21; Mark 11.23).

12.10 – Thomas 114   D

**See, I shall lead her
so that I will make her great as a male
that she may become a living spirit
resembling you males.
For every woman
who considers herself great as a male
will enter the kingdom of heaven.**

Peter had suggested that Mary should not be allowed to accompany them since women were unworthy of life. This derogatory remark in line with the low view of women in the ancient world earned a severe rebuke from Jesus, who has restored women to their rightful position as equals with men, as

Paul realized: 'There is . . . neither male nor female; for you are all one in Christ Jesus' (Galatians 3.28).

Thomas 114 has usually been translated as, 'I will make her male'; but the Coptic verb means 'make great', 'glorify', 'exalt', rather than simply 'make'.[4] If this were a genuine saying, Jesus would be encouraging women to abandon any inferiority complex they may have and to regard themselves as the equals of men. In any case, Jesus has already exalted them to such a status.

---

5 Christian Life and Witness

12.11 – Thomas 24   B

Let whoever has ears, hear.
Within a person of light there is light
which lights the whole world.
When this light does not shine
there is darkness.

The light-giving quality of those who have been illuminated by Jesus is also stressed in the Sermon on the Mount (Matthew 5.14, 16).[5]

12.12 – Thomas 25   A

Love your brother as yourself;
guard him as the apple of your eye.

In the synoptic gospels (Matthew 19.19; 22.39; Mark 12.31; Luke 10.27), it is love of neighbour that is commanded by Jesus, but in John 13.34 and 15.12 the disciples are commanded to love one another (compare 1 John 2.10). *Thomas* 25 is closer to the sentiment expressed in John's Gospel and letters, where the love command seems to be limited to one's fellow-Christians. The apple or pupil of the eye was regarded as being very tender and precious and as such required the utmost care (Deuteronomy 32.10; Psalm 17.8; Proverbs 7.2).[6]

12.13 – Thomas 26 A

**You see the speck in your brother's eye
but fail to see the log in your own eye.
Once you have cast the log out of your eye,
then you will see clearly
to take the speck from your brother's eye.**

This is a shorter version of the saying found in Matthew 7.3–5 and Luke 6.41f. (Q). It reduces two questions and a statement to two statements. Since the second of the two questions seems to repeat the first one, the form of the saying in *Thomas* could be more primitive.

12.14 – Thomas 32 A

**A city built on a high mountain and fortified
cannot fall nor can it be hidden.**

This expanded version occurs also in Oxyrhynchus Papyrus 1 (6.7). Since it is found in two editions of Tatian's *Diatessaron* (**8.13**)[7], it must go back at least to the second century AD – probably even to Jewish-Christian tradition in the first century. Not only so; but on account of poetic parallelism – 'built and fortified . . . cannot fall or be hidden' – it may even be preferable to the shorter form in Matthew 5.14. In the parable of the two houses with which the Sermon on the Mount concludes (Matthew 7.24–27; compare Luke 6.47–49), the house built upon the rock 'did not fall because it had been founded upon the rock'.

Even the context of the saying in Matthew 5.14 is suspect. There it seems to convey the same meaning as those about disciples being the light of the world and about placing lamps on lampstands. Christians must show up to the best advantage since all eyes will be upon them. In *Thomas*, on the other hand, the saying is placed before those about preaching from the housetops and about lamps on lampstands (*Thomas* 33 – 12.15). This suggests a different meaning. It may be that the saying in *Thomas* 32 should also be interpreted with reference to preaching.

Whatever its original form and meaning, a saying about a city built on a hill is attested by at least two independent witnesses and probably goes back to Jesus and can therefore be regarded as authentic (A).[8]

12.15 – Thomas 33   A

What you hear in both ears
preach from the housetops;
for no one lights a lamp
and places it under a grain-measure
or places it in a hidden place
but sets it on the lampstand
so that all who go in and out may see its light.

There is a version of the first part in Oxyrhynchus Papyrus 1 (6.8), but the text is so fragmentary that it is of little use. As we have already seen, one suggested restoration of that text does not fit in with *Thomas* 33, which is more in line with Matthew 10.27 and Luke 12.3 (Q). The Coptic text translated 'in both ears' reads literally 'in your ear in your ear'. This could be an example of dittography, that is, a scribe writing twice what should have been written only once.[9]

The grain-measure under which the clay lamp is placed in the small, windowless peasant house in order to avoid an unpleasant smell as it is being extinguished is also referred to in Matthew 5.15 and Mark 4.21. However, another picture is also presented in *Thomas* 33 as well as in Tatian (**8.13**) and in Luke 8.16 and 11.33, where the model may be that of the larger Hellenistic house also to be found in Palestine. A lamp placed in the vestibule would give light to all who enter and leave. This may be an authentic touch.[10]

12.16 – Thomas 35   A

It is not possible
to enter the house of a strong man

**and take him by force without binding his hands.
Then one can ransack his house.**

There are parallels to this saying in all three synoptic gospels. It
agrees with Mark 3.27 in being a statement; in Matthew 12.29,
this is put in the form of a question; while Luke 11.21 and 22 has
a different version in the form of a parable. Since the saying was
probably in Q as well as in Mark and *Thomas*, we can grade it A
as being in three independent sources.[11] *Thomas* 35 is clearly
independent of Mark. The phrase, 'take by force', is similar to
Luke's version, 'attacks and conquers'.

12.17 – Thomas 36   A

**Take no anxious thought
from morning until evening
and from evening until morning
for what you shall put on.**

While *Thomas* 36 has only the reference to clothing, perhaps in
view of the content of *Thomas* 37 (12.7), the Greek version from
Oxyrhynchus (6.16 and 17) speaks of three things about which
one should not worry anxiously, as do Matthew 6.25ff. and Luke
12.22ff. – food, clothing and the span of one's life. In *Thomas* 36,
the addition of 'from evening until morning' suggests lying
awake all night worrying about what to put on the next day.

12.18 – Thomas 40   A

**A vine has been planted without the Father
and, as it is not established,
it will be uprooted and destroyed.**

This seems to have come independently of the synoptic tradition
from a saying of Jesus that also lies behind Matthew 15.13: 'Any
plant which my heavenly Father did not plant will be uprooted.'
In John 15.1, on the other hand, it is Jesus himself who is the
vine. This declaration is followed immediately by a similar

warning to that contained in *Thomas* 40 – 'Every branch of mine that bears no fruit, he takes away, and every branch that does bear fruit he prunes, that it may bear more fruit' (John 15.2).

12.19 – Thomas *41* A

To him who has in his hand it shall be given
and from him who does not have
shall be taken away
even the small quantity that he has.

To the similar saying found in the synoptic gospels, *Thomas* has added two phrases – 'in his hand' and 'even the small quantity that he has'. In the New Testament, it is found in two different places – as part of Jesus' explanation of his use of parables in Mark 4.25 (Matthew 13.12; Luke 8.18) and at the conclusion of the parable of the talents (Matthew 25.29) or pounds (Luke 19.26). It may have been a floating saying not firmly anchored in the tradition, or Jesus may have uttered it on more than one occasion. It must have been a well-known saying in early Christian circles, since it was probably in Q as well as in Mark and *Thomas*, where it is one of five sayings almost identical with synoptic sayings.[12]

12.20 – Thomas *42* A

Become passers by.

This is the shortest of all the sayings in *Thomas*, but its meaning is not altogether clear. It could be taken as advocating a life of celibacy such as was characteristic of the early Syrian Church. On the other hand, it could simply be a call to recognize the transitory nature of this present life. In this case, the saying would echo the reminder found in the New Testament that we are strangers and exiles on earth (Hebrews 11.13; 1 Peter 2.11). World renunciation occurs also in *Thomas* 27 (10.34); 56 (10.7); 110 (10.6) and in the Arabic bridge saying (17.30). It could well be primitive and authentic.[13]

12.21 – Thomas 45 A

They do not harvest grapes from thorns
nor do they gather figs from thistles.
A good man brings forth good out of his treasure,
an evil man brings forth evil things
out of his evil treasure,
which is in his heart, and speaks evil things.
For out of the abundance of the heart
he brings forth evil things.

The first saying here has slight variations from Matthew 7.16 and Luke 6.44 (Q). The second has a few additions to Matthew 12.35 – 'which is in his heart' (compare Luke 6.45 – 'of his heart'), 'and speaks evil things' and 'he bring forth evil things'. All three are found in various editions of the *Diatessaron* (**8.13**).

12.22 – Thomas 47 A

It is impossible for a man to mount two horses
and to stretch two bows
and it is impossible for a slave
to serve two masters.
Otherwise, he will honour the one
and offend the other.
No man drinks old wine
and immediately desires to drink new wine;
and they do not put new wine
into old wineskins lest they burst
and they do not put old wine
into a new wineskin lest it spoil it.
They do not sew an old patch on a new garment
because there would come a rent.

The two impossible feats of mounting two horses and stretching two bows are not found in the Q version of the next saying about serving two masters (Matthew 6.24; Luke 16.13), though Matthew seems to have thought of Jesus as having performed the first impossible feat on Palm Sunday by his introduction of a second animal into the story – 'They brought the ass and the colt . . . and he sat upon them' (Matthew 21.7), perhaps on account of some misunderstanding of the Hebrew parallelism in Zechariah 9.9 – 'riding on an ass, on a colt the foal of an ass'. There is an interesting Arabic parallel to the saying about serving two masters which speaks about the difficulty of pleasing two wives (17.28).

The preference for old wine found as an addition to the parable of the wine and the wineskins both in *Thomas* 47 and in Luke 5.39 is unfortunate since the parable stresses the incompatibility of new wine (as a symbol of the new age) with old. The addition emphasizes the superiority of the old, which is not the lesson that Jesus is teaching in the parable but the exact opposite. This addition does not necessarily mean that *Thomas* was dependent on Luke. Both may have been drawing upon the same oral tradition or written source.[14]

The absurdity of the idea of putting new wine into old wineskins is found in Matthew 9.17; Mark 2.22 and Luke 5.37. The meaning is that the new and old do not mix, whether it be wine or cloth (as in what follows in *Thomas* 47 and precedes in the synoptics) or religion. In the end, Christianity and Judaism are incompatible, even though the former grew out of the latter. One cannot be a professing Jew and a professing Christian at the same time, though of course, it is possible to be a Jewish Christian or a Christian Jew.

12.23 – Thomas 48   B

If two make peace with each other in one house
they shall say to the mountain:
'Be moved', and it shall be moved.

Here, reconciliation replaces faith (Matthew 17.20; 1 Corinthians 13.2) as the force which removes mountains. The theme of unity runs through *Thomas* (compare Matthew 18.19). There is a more developed form of this saying in *Thomas* 106 (12.9).

12.24 – Thomas 50   D

If they say to you:
'From where have you originated?'
say to them: 'We have come from the light
where the light has originated through itself.
It stood and revealed itself in their image.'
If they say to you: 'Who are you?'
say: 'We are his sons
and we are the elect of the living Father.'
If they ask you:
'What is the sign of your Father in you?'
say to them: 'It is movement together with rest.'

In *Thomas* 49 (9.19), there is a reference to the kingdom from
which believers have come and to which they return. Now we
are told that its nature is light. This is a constant feature not
only in the Fourth Gospel and in First John, but also in the Dead
Sea Scrolls. Both John and the Essenes speak of a dualism
between light and darkness, created by, and subservient to, the
one God of the universe. Not only is God light (1 John 1.5) but
the life that was in the pre-existent Logos is the true light of
human beings (John 1.4f., 9; 8.12). So Jesus tells his disciples in
the Sermon on the Mount that they are the light of the world
(Matthew 5.14; compare *Thomas* 24 – 12.11).

As sons of light (Luke 16.8; John 12.36; 1 Thessalonians 5.5),
disciples are also sons of the living Father. As the elect or God's
chosen ones, they are moving towards rest, a recurring theme
in *Thomas* and in the New Testament (Matthew 11.28–30;
Hebrews 3.11—4.11). The rest to which Christians are moving is
already present in so far as the kingdom or rule of God is both
here in this world as the result of the coming of Jesus and also
something to be fully realized in the world to come. This paradox
is expressed in *Thomas* 50 in terms of movement together with
rest. This is the sign of the living Father in the disciples of Jesus.

12.25 – Thomas 62 A

*I tell my mysteries to those
[who are worthy of my] mysteries.
What your right hand will do,
let not your left hand know what it does.*

The first part is similar to Matthew 13.11; Mark 4.11; Luke 8.10. The second is advice given in the Sermon on the Mount within the context of instructions about almsgiving (Matthew 6.3).

12.26 – Thomas 73 A

*The harvest is indeed great
but the labourers are few;
beg the lord to send labourers into the harvest.*

This is virtually identical with Matthew 9.37f. and Luke 10.2 (Q).

12.27 – Thomas 74 C

*Lord, there are many around the well
but there is no one in it.*

This may not actually be a saying of Jesus but of the person with whom he is engaged in conversation. Following upon what Jesus has just said in *Thomas* 73 (12.26), someone in his audience uses another agricultural metaphor to press home the point that, while many are waiting for the water that Jesus can give, no one has taken the decision to drink it.[15]

12.28 – Thomas 93 A

*Do not give what is holy to the dogs
lest they throw them on the dungheap.
Do not throw pearls before pigs
lest they . . .*

To the first clause found also in Matthew 7.6 has been added the second clause (not found in Matthew), which balances the fourth clause, lost in *Thomas* but completed in Matthew:

> **Do not give what is holy to the dogs**
> **and do not throw your pearls before pigs**
> **lest they trample them underfoot and turn to attack you.**

The original saying may have had all four clauses, though it is odd to think of 'dogs' being able to 'throw' things on to the dungheap. Yet 'dogs' is obviously being used in a metaphorical sense of people who are not fit to receive the message of the gospel, whether they be Gentiles or sinners or both.[16]

12.29 – Thomas 100   A

> **Give the things of Caesar to Caesar,**
> **give the things of God to God,**
> **and give me what is mine.**

This was the response of Jesus when asked about paying taxes to the Roman overlords of Palestine (Matthew 22.15–22; Mark 12.13–17; Luke 20.20–26). To the saying as found in the synoptic gospels there has been added the third clause about giving Jesus what belongs to him. It is not stated what this is.[17] It should not be assumed that God is being subordinated to Jesus or that this represents a gnosticizing expansion of the original saying.[18] There is a possible introduction to this response in Egerton Papyrus 2 (5.6).[19]

12.30 – Thomas 108   c

> **Whoever drinks from my mouth**
> **will become as I am;**
> **I myself will become he**
> **and hidden things will be revealed to him.**

This recalls sayings from John's Gospel – 'If anyone thirsts, let him come to me and drink' (John 7.37); 'Abide in me and I in you' (John 15.4) – and Paul's conception of a Christian as a person who is 'in Christ' (2 Corinthians 5.17).

---

6 The Cost of Discipleship

12.31 – Thomas *55*   A

Whoever does not hate his father and his mother
will not be able to be my disciple;
and whoever does not hate
his brothers and his sisters
and does not take up his cross as I have done
will not be worthy of me.

The first part of this saying with the addition of 'as I do' is found in *Thomas* 101 (12.32). There is also a parallel in Matthew 10.37 and Luke 14.26 (Q), though Matthew 10.37 has 'loves more' instead of 'does not hate' and Luke 14.26 includes wife and children. *Thomas* 55 counsels breaking with the family we came from but not the family we founded. This may seem strange in view of the extreme asceticism found elsewhere in *Thomas*. However, those who are solitary (*monachos*) or single (*oua ouot*) would not have wife and children to hate (**8.16; 8.17**).

The reference to taking up one's cross is found in Mark 8.34, followed by Matthew 16.24 and Luke 9.23 (where 'daily' is added) and also in Q (Matthew 10.38; Luke 14.27). It is a vivid reminder to the disciples of the constant danger of crucifixion, a common method of capital punishment in Palestine under the Romans. It is not necessarily a reference to the death of Jesus himself. The disciples had to be prepared at all times to make the ultimate sacrifice, as Jesus himself was.

12.32 – Thomas *101*   A

Whoever does not hate his father
and his mother as I do
will not be able to be my disciple.

> **Whoever does not love his father**
> **and his mother as I do**
> **will not be able to be my disciple.**
> **For my mother . . .**
> **but my true mother gave me life.**

This opens with a doublet of the first part of *Thomas* 55 (12.31) with the addition of the phrase, 'as I do'. Then there is a development of *Thomas* 55. Though the papyrus is damaged towards the end of the saying, it is clear that the final statement points to a solution to the paradox in the first two. A disciple is expected to abandon his natural family for his true or spiritual family, from whom he has gained eternal life.

12.33 – Thomas 82   A

> **He who is near me is near the fire;**
> **and he who is far from me**
> **is far from the kingdom.**

The first half contains a stern warning about the cost of discipleship. It is echoed in Mark 9.49, where we are told that 'every one will be salted with fire'. The complete saying contains a paradox with a double warning. It is dangerous to be near Jesus, but it is equally and even far more so to be far from him; for that spells ultimate disaster. It is to be far from the kingdom and from eternal life. Origen (16.20) also quotes this saying but cannot remember where he found it. His source could have been *Thomas* 82.[20]

Part Four

A Handful of Silver

Part Four

Handful of Silver

CHAPTER THIRTEEN

Fanciful Tales

1 Infancy Gospels and Legendary Letter

In the canonical gospels, little is recorded about the early life of
Jesus. Apart from the birth stories in the two opening chapters of
Matthew and Luke, including the story of the visit to the temple
when he was twelve years old, nothing is known about him,
except that 'he increased in wisdom and stature and in favour
with God and man' (Luke 2.52). Where history fails, legend has
taken over. There are several infancy gospels purporting to deal
with his birth and childhood; for example, the *Infancy Gospel of
Thomas*, an *Arabic Infancy Gospel* and a *Latin Infancy Gospel*.
There is also a legendary letter supposed to have been written by
Jesus to Abgar in response to a request to visit Edessa.[1]

Most of these sources are of little historical or theological
value. They contain stories of miracles and other fanciful tales.
The boy Jesus is shown as a prodigy at school, instructing his
teachers in the mysteries of the alphabet. Incorporated within
these tales, there are sayings attributed to Jesus. In this chapter,
we shall look briefly at the *Infancy Gospel of Thomas* and consider
the legendary letter of Jesus to King Abgar.

2 Infancy Gospel of Thomas

As we have already noted (**8.2**), the *Infancy Gospel of Thomas*
has to be carefully distinguished from the Coptic *Gospel of
Thomas*. Unlike its namesake, it contains fanciful stories about
the boy Jesus between the ages of five and twelve years. Only two

of those which include alleged sayings are included here. Both of them involve legendary miracles.

13.1 – 2.4 D

Joseph called out to Jesus:
'Why are you doing these things
which ought not to be done on the sabbath?'
Jesus clapped his hands
and called out to the sparrows:
'Be off!'
And the sparrows took flight and flew away chirping.

This incident is said to have taken place when Jesus was five years old. While playing with other children beside a brook one sabbath, he fashioned these twelve sparrows from clay. A Jew reported this profanation of the sabbath to Joseph, who came and rebuked him.

13.2 – 10.2 C

Arise now! Split the wood and remember me.

With these words, the child Jesus is said to have healed a young man who had injured his foot with an axe. As he continued the task of chopping wood, he should remember the person who had healed him. Even though this is a fanciful tale, it could incorporate part of a genuine saying (hence graded C) found in more complete form in the Greek and Coptic versions of the *Gospel of Thomas* (6.5; *Thomas* 77 – 11.17) – 'Split the wood (a piece of wood), and I am there'.

---

3 Letter to Abgar the Great

13.3 D

Happy are you,
who believed in me without having seen me.
For it is written concerning me
that those who have seen me
will not believe in me
and that those who have not seen me
will believe and live.
But concerning what you have written to me
that I should come to you
I must fulfil here all for which I was sent
and afterwards be taken up again
to him who sent me.
When I have been taken up
I shall send to you one of my disciples
so that he may heal your affliction
and give life to you
and to those who are with you.

This is the legendary letter written by Jesus to Abgar the Great, King of Edessa in Syria (AD 9–46), in response to a request to come to Syria to heal him. Jesus declined the invitation since he had enough to do in Palestine but promised to send one of his disciples instead. After the ascension, Judas Thomas sent Thaddaeus, one of the seventy-two, to Edessa as an apostle. A copy of this legendary letter was inscribed on stone and fixed to the Harran Gate through which the letter was believed to have been brought into the city; and the gate was kept closed. Copies of the letter have been found in Asia Minor, Egypt and Macedonia. It was revered in Spain and worn as amulets in Ireland before the time of the Norman Conquest.[2]

Whether or not this correspondence is genuine, it points to the early establishment of Christianity in Edessa, perhaps even to the conversion of Abgar the Great. However, it seems more likely that the first Christian king of Edessa was Abgar IX (AD 179–86) and that the background of his time has been read back into the time of Jesus; but there is reason to think that Abgar the Great was a historical figure and that he was a Jew from Palestine. Even if the correspondence is not genuine, it does point to the possibility that Christianity had reached Edessa before the end of the first century.[3]

CHAPTER FOURTEEN

Apostolic Writings

1 Apostolic Authority

Within the New Testament, various books that clearly had the authority of the apostles have been collected. As we have seen (1.5), this was one of the tests that was applied in the long process of deciding which writings were worthy of a place in the canon of the New Testament.

In addition to authentic apostolic writings, several works have survived outside the New Testament which bear the name of an apostle but are clearly pseudepigraphal, that is, written under false names. None of these are of much value apart from the *Gospel of Thomas*, which we have already considered in detail (chapters 8 to 12). Many sayings attributed to Jesus elsewhere look like fabrications, but there are a few that are identical with, or are similar to, those in the canonical gospels.

2 The *Gospel of Peter*

In 1886, a fragment of a gospel claiming to have the authority of Peter was discovered at Akhmim in Egypt in the tomb of an eighth-century Christian monk. It begins in the middle of the passion narrative and ends in the middle of an account of an appearance of the risen Jesus at the Lake of Tiberias. According to Eusebius, the fourth-century historian, the use of this gospel in church was discouraged by Serapion, Bishop of Antioch (second/third century), because it seemed to teach that Jesus was not fully human.[1]

14.1 – 5.19 D

My power, o power, you left me in the lurch.

These final words of Jesus on the cross are a variant of Mark
15.34 and Matthew 27.46 – 'My God, my God, why did you
forsake me?' Both in Peter and in Matthew and Mark, the Greek
verb is almost the same one as that found in Luke 10.40, where
Martha rebukes Jesus for allowing Mary to leave her alone to
prepare the meal. This version of the last words of Jesus seems to
be an attempt to avoid any possible misunderstanding about
God's having forsaken Jesus. It was only power that left him, not
God.[2]

---

3 The *Preaching of Peter*

Clement of Alexandria (**16.6**) quotes several times from this
document, which he clearly regarded as having been composed
by Peter. Origen (**16.9**) did not share this high opinion of the
work and doubted its authenticity.

14.2 – From Clement, Miscellanies 6.5.43 D

If now any one of Israel wishes to repent
and through my name to believe in God,
his sins will be forgiven him.
And after twelve years go out into the world
that no one may say, 'We have not heard'.

Twelve years is the period during which, according to this
document, the apostles were told by Jesus to concentrate on
preaching to the Jews. Only thereafter were they to go to the rest
of the world to proclaim the gospel (Matthew 28.19; Luke
24.47).

14.3 – From *Clement*, Miscellanies 6.6.48 D

I have chosen you twelve
because I judged you worthy to be my disciples
(whom the Lord wished).
And I sent them,
of whom I was persuaded
that they would be true apostles,
into the world to proclaim
to people in all the world
the joyous message
that they may know that there is only one God
and to reveal what future happenings
there would be through belief on me (Christ),
to the end that those who hear and believe me
may be saved:
and that those who believe not may testify
that they have heard it
and not be able to excuse themselves saying,
'We have not heard'.

The first sentence is echoed in a shorter saying quoted from the *Gospel of the Nazaraeans* by Eusebius (15.5). The final words are paralleled in Romans 10.14, where Paul asks how people can believe in one of whom they have not heard.

---

4 The Acts of Peter

This apocryphal book was composed in Greek in the second half of the second century AD, but it is known to us mainly from a sixth- or seventh-century Latin manuscript.[3] One of the legends it contains tells how, when Peter was fleeing in disguise from Rome, he had a vision of the risen Lord going in the opposite direction. Peter asked him, 'Lord, where are you going (*Quo vadis*)?' Jesus replied, 'I am coming to Rome to be crucified.' Peter took this as a sign that he should return to the city to face martyrdom.

14.4 – 10 B

Those who are with me have not understood me.

Marcellus, a leading member of the Church at Rome, abandoned the faith, led astray by Simon Magus, as were some of the people of Samaria (Acts 8.9). Later, he came back under the influence of Peter. He begged Peter to pray for him, reminding him of the saying of Jesus about faith like a grain of mustard seed and of how Peter had lost faith upon the water. Marcellus also recalled this saying of Jesus. If even Peter could doubt and then be reinstated, surely he, Marcellus, could likewise be forgiven.

Over and over again in the gospels, Jesus complains about the failure of his disciples to understand him, as in Mark 4.13, where they fail to comprehend the meaning of the parable of the sower and the soils, and in Mark 8.17, where Jesus complains about their hardened hearts or closed minds.[4]

14.5 – 38 C

Unless you make what is on the right hand
as what is on the left
and what is on the left hand
as what is on the right
and what is above as what is below
and what is behind as what is before,
you will not recognize the kingdom.

Peter is said to have quoted these words of Jesus after he had, at is own request, been crucified head-downwards. It is only when one turns round that what was formerly on one's right is on one's left. So this would appear to be a graphic call to repentance as in Jesus' challenge to turn and become as children in Matthew 18.3. Conversion means turning round.[5]

---

5 The *Gospel of Philip*

The *Gospel of Philip* may have been originally composed in Greek but survives only in a single Coptic version. This immediately follows the *Gospel of Thomas* in the second codex found in the clay jar at Chenoboskion in December 1945 and so forms part of the Nag Hammadi Library (**7.2**). It is obviously a later document from the second half of the third century and shows clear gnostic influence. A collection of statements about sacraments and ethics, it also contains fifteen sayings of Jesus, some of which are already known to us from the New Testament – a reference to the Lord's Prayer and direct quotations from Matthew 3.15; 6.6; 15.13; Mark 15.34; John 6.53; 8.34. There are only eight sayings not recorded in the canonical gospels.[6]

Of the eight sayings not recorded in the canonical gospels, most are of doubtful authenticity and so are graded D. Since it is difficult to make sense out of some of them, only six are quoted below.

14.6 – 56.1–3 D

From every house,
bring into the house of the Father;
but do not take anything in the house of the Father
nor carry it off.

Some have seen echoes here of the saying of Jesus in John 14.2 about there being many rooms in his Father's house and of the synoptic account of the cleansing of the temple, where Jesus rebuked those who were using the temple court as a thoroughfare for carrying goods (Mark 11.16)[7]

14.7 – 58.11–14 D

You who have joined the perfect, light,
with the Holy Spirit,
unite the angels with us also, the images.

Although this is said to have been part of what Jesus himself prayed one day in the course of the thanksgiving, whatever that was, it looks more like a prayer to Jesus as the one who, by coming as a human being, united light, which is seen as perfection, like the angels, with earthly things, which are only images of what is true.[8]

14.8 – 59.26–27 D

Ask your mother and she will give you of the things which are another's.

This is said to be the reply given by Jesus to a disciple who asked him to give him something of this world. This may be a reference to the Holy Spirit, who would give to him something far superior to worldly things.

14.9 – 63.28–30 D

Even so has the Son of man come [as a dyer].

Earlier in this document, God is said to be a dyer whose dyes are immortal. Those who are dipped in them through baptism become immortal. Now Jesus may be comparing himself to a dyer. He is reported to have entered the dye works of someone called Levi, taken seventy-two different colours, thrown them into the vat and taken them all out white, the colour of purity.

Two different restorations of the text have been suggested: either, 'to take away defects' or 'as a dyer'. The first of these could be compared with John 1.29, where John the Baptist pointed to Jesus as the lamb of God who takes away the sin of the world. In either case, the saying could have a baptismal reference.

There is a legend in the *Arabic Infancy Gospel* (**13.1**) about the child Jesus taking cloths out of a cauldron dyed in any colour which the dyer wished. If both stories have come from a common source, their varying details indicate that they have been adapted for different purposes.[9]

14.10 – 64.10–12   D

Happy is he who is before he came into being.
For he who is, has been and shall be.

This would appear to be a beatitude on Jesus himself as the pre-
existent one, as in *Thomas* 19 (9.18). Compare John 8.58:
'Before Abraham was I am.'

14.11 – 74.25–26   D

Some have entered the kingdom of heaven laughing
and they have come out . . . [a Christian].

The rest of this saying survives only in isolated words. One can
only guess its meaning. The reference may be to true believers
who can laugh because they despise the material world. It is also
possible that there is a baptismal reference. Those who joyfully
accept the sacrament realize that the end of this mortal life is an
occasion for joy, not mourning.[10]

CHAPTER FIFTEEN

Jewish Christians and Egyptians

1 Various Gospels

There were probably three Jewish-Christian Gospels in the first
few centuries AD: the *Gospel of the Nazaraeans* (**15.2**), the *Gospel
of the Ebionites* (**15.3**) and the *Gospel of the Hebrews* (**15.4**).
There was also a *Gospel of the Egyptians* (**15.5**). Very little can be
said about these gospels or who wrote them because none of
them has survived. They are known to us only from fragments
quoted by early Christian writers such as Justin Martyr (about
AD 100 to about AD 165 – **16.4**), Clement of Alexandria (about
AD 150 to about AD 215 – **16.6**), Origen (about AD 185 to about
AD 254 – **16.9**) and Jerome in the fourth century (**2.1**).[1]

2 The *Gospel of the Nazaraeans*

This document seems to have been written in Syriac or Aramaic
and to have been roughly identical in content with Matthew's
Gospel. Extra details have been added in certain narratives.

15.1 – From Jerome c

**Wherein have I sinned
that I should go and be baptized by him?
Unless what I have said is (a sin of) ignorance.**

This, according to Jerome, was the reply given by Jesus to his
mother and brothers when they suggested that he should go with

them to be baptized by John the Baptist for remission of sins. Similarly, in *Thomas* 104 (10.23), Jesus professed sinlessness when invited by the disciples to pray and fast with them.

15.2 – From Jerome B

Our bread of tomorrow give us today.

In his commentary on Matthew 6.11, Jerome gives this as an alternative rendering for the Greek word usually translated into English as 'daily', though he himself gives the meaning as being 'essential to existence'. In classical Greek, a very similar word meant 'following'. So it is possible that Jesus told his disciples to pray for bread for the following day, that is, tomorrow. William Barclay translated the fourth petition in the Lord's Prayer as: 'Give us today our bread for the coming day' (Matthew 6.11); 'Give us each day bread for the coming day' (Luke 11.3).[2] This neatly preserves the possible ambiguity in the Greek word. If prayed early in the day, it is today's bread for which we ask. If prayed later in the day, it is bread for the next day.

15.3 – From Jerome B

If your brother sins with a word and makes amends
receive him seven times in a day.
Yes; even seventy times seven.
For in the prophets also
the sinful word was found
even after they had been anointed
by the Holy Spirit.

Jerome quotes this extended version of Matthew 18.21 and 22 with two of the additions found in Luke 17.4 – 'makes amends' and 'in a day'. Two extra features are unique to this extended version – 'with a word' and the fact that the prophets also were guilty of speaking sinful words. If even such great and good people were not immune from such sins, one should be prepared to forgive lesser mortals.[3]

155

15.4 – From Origen   B

The other of the two rich men said to him:
'Master, what good thing must I do that I may live?'
He said to him:
'Man, fulfil the law and the prophets.'
He answered him: 'That have I done.'
He said to him:
'Go and sell what you possess
and distribute it among the poor
and then come and follow me.'
But the rich man began to scratch his head
and the saying did not please him.
And the Lord said to him: 'How can you say,
I have fulfilled the law and the prophets?
For it stands written in the law:
Love your neighbour as yourself;
and behold many of your brethren, sons of Abraham,
are dirty and die of hunger
and your house is full of many good things
and nothing at all comes from it to them.'
And he turned and said to Simon, his disciple,
who was sitting by him:
'Simon, son of Jona,
it is easier for a camel
to go through the eye of a needle
than for a rich man
to enter the kingdom of heaven.'

This extended version of the story of the rich man (Matthew 19.16–22; Mark 10.17–22; Luke 18.18–23) is given by Origen (**16.9**) in his commentary on Matthew. There is nothing in this account that could not have been genuine, even though a second man is introduced into the narrative. Extra vivid touches like scratching the head lend credence to the story. The point is clearly made that it is not riches themselves but their selfish use that is condemned by Jesus.[4]

15.5 – From Eusebius c

**I chose for myself the most worthy:
the most worthy are those
whom the Father in heaven has given me.**

In John 17.6, the disciples are those whom the Father had given to Jesus: but in John 15.16, Jesus declares that he had chosen the disciples and that they had not chosen him. Their worthiness did not necessarily enter into the choice, whether it was made by the Father or by Jesus. According to Clement of Alexandria, a much longer version of this saying was to be found in the *Preaching of Peter* (14.3).

---

3 The *Gospel of the Ebionites*

The *Gospel of the Ebionites* is the modern name given to a gospel used by the Ebionites, a Jewish-Christian sect. This gospel appears to have been an abridged and corrupted version of Matthew. Epiphanius, fourth-century Bishop of Salamis, quotes from it in his principal work, *Refutation of all the Heresies*, but incorrectly calls it the *Gospel of the Hebrews*.

15.6 – From Epiphanius c

**As I passed along the Lake of Tiberias,
I chose John and James the sons of Zebedee,
and Simon and Andrew and Thaddaeus
and Simon the Zealot and Judas Iscariot,
and you alone, Matthew, I called
as you sat at the receipt of custom
and you followed me.
You therefore I will to be twelve apostles
for a testimony to Israel.**

According to Epiphanius, Jesus entered into Simon Peter's house in Capernaum and spoke these words.

15.7 – From Epiphanius A

**Let it be: for it is fitting
that everything should be fulfilled.**

This response to John's unwillingness to baptize Jesus is clearly
from Matthew 3.15. According to the *Gospel of the Nazaraeans*
(15.1), Jesus had previously refused to accompany his mother
and his brothers for baptism.

15.8 – From Epiphanius A

**Who are my mother and my brothers?
These are my brothers and mother and sisters,
who do the will of my Father.**

This is an obvious parallel to Matthew 12.48–50.

15.9 – From Epiphanius D

**I have come to do away with sacrifices
and if you do not cease from sacrificing
the wrath of God will not cease from you.**

This seems to contradict Jesus' declaration that he had not come
to abolish the law and the prophets (Matthew 5.17). In John
3.36, it is said that the wrath of God rests upon the person who
does not obey the Son.

4 The Gospel of the Hebrews

The Jewish-Christian character of this gospel is revealed by the
prominence it gives to James, the brother of Jesus, who was
leader of the early Jerusalem church (*Thomas* 12 – 12.1). It may
have been composed in the first half of the second century. Egypt
has been suggested as its place of origin since Clement of
Alexandria and Origen are the chief witnesses to its existence.
Some of the details quoted from it sound mythical.

15.10 – From Origen and Jerome   D

**Even so did my mother, the Holy Spirit,
take me by one of my hairs
and carry me away on to the great mountain Tabor.**

Both Origen and Jerome quote this unlikely account of the temptation of Jesus in various places in their commentaries, though Origen does preface it with the remark, 'And if any accept the *Gospel of the Hebrews*, here the Saviour says . . .'.

15.11 – From Clement   C

**He who wonders shall reign
and he who has reigned shall rest.**

Quoted by Clement in his *Miscellanies* 2.9.45, this and the following saying are found amalgamated and with slight differences in *Thomas* 2 (10.2) and also in Oxyrhynchus Papyrus 654 (6.10).

15.12 – From Clement   C

**He who seeks will not find rest until he finds;
and he who has found shall wonder;
and he who has wondered shall reign;
and he who has reigned shall rest.**

This longer form of the previous saying is quoted by Clement in *Miscellanies* 5.14.96.

15.13 – From Jerome   B

**Never be joyful
except when you look upon your brother with love.**

The Latin version of this saying found in Jerome's commentary on Ephesians 5.4 is ambiguous. One could translate the last clause as, 'except when you have seen that your brother is in love'. This is unlikely to be the meaning. The brother referred to is a fellow-countryman, as in Matthew 5.22 ('Every one who is angry with his brother . . .'); 18.15 ('If your brother sins against you . . .'); Leviticus 19.17 ('You shall not hate your brother in your heart . . .'). This otherwise unknown saying is far more positive than any of these others and sounds authentic. It corresponds to the brotherly love enjoined by Jesus upon his disciples in John 15.12: '. . . love one another as I have loved you'. In the previous verse, Jesus links such love with joy. Obedience to the command of Jesus to love one's brother brings complete joy (John 15.11). In Galatians 5.22, Paul declares that love and joy are the first two ingredients in the fruit of the Spirit.[5]

15.14 – From Jerome   c

'Bring a table and bread!'
And immediately it is added:
he took the bread, blessed it
and brake it and gave it
to James the Just and said:
'My brother, eat your bread
for the Son of man is risen
from among those who sleep.'

Jerome writes that this comes from the *Gospel of the Hebrews*, which he had recently translated into Greek and Latin and which Origen frequently used. These words were said to have been addressed by the risen Jesus to his brother, James (12.1), who had sworn that he would not eat anything until he had seen Jesus alive.

---

5 The *Gospel of the Egyptians*

The chief source of our knowledge of this gospel is Clement of Alexandria (about AD 150 to about AD 215 – **16.6**), who quotes from it in the course of discussions about marriage and sexuality.

Origen (about AD 185 to about AD 254 – **16.9**) also refers to it, though it is quite clear that by his time it was not recognized by the Church.

15.15 – From Clement   D

**When you tread upon the garments of shame
and when the two are one
and the male with the female
neither male nor female.**

This echoes the idea of contempt for, and annulment of, sexuality found in certain sayings in *Thomas* (12.5–10), though, as in *Thomas* 37 (12.7), the reference to treading on garments could be a reference to baptism. Theodore of Mopsuestia (about AD 350 to 428) witnesses to the Syrian baptismal ritual of the person about to be baptized taking off outer garments and standing barefoot with outstretched arms on sackcloth as a sign of penitence. The whole saying quoted here by Clement (*Miscellanies* 3.13.92) is a response to a question from Salome as to when the things about which she was asking would be known.

15.16 – From Clement   D

**When Salome asked,
'How long will death have power?'
the Lord answered,
'So long as you women bear children.'**

Clement (*Miscellanies* 3.45) interprets this as meaning not that life is bad and creation evil, but as teaching the sequence of nature.

15.17 – From Clement   D

I have come to undo the works of the female.

Clement (*Miscellanies* 3.63) is arguing against encratites (**3.10;** **8.14**), who, he declares, attribute this saying to Jesus in support of their views rejecting marriage (**16.6**).

CHAPTER SIXTEEN

Early Christian Writers

1 Introduction

In this chapter, we shall be looking at sayings found in early Christian writers and writings from the late first century to the fourth century.

From the first century, there is a letter ascribed to Clement of Rome and written about AD 96 (**16.2** – 16.1). This is followed by a mid-second-century sermon known as *Second Clement* (**16.3** – 16.2–7). Also from the second century come the writings of Justin Martyr (**16.4** – 16.8, 9) and Irenaeus (**16.5** – 16.10).

Out of Africa in the second and third centuries came the writings of Clement, head of the catechetical school at Alexandria (**16.6** – 16.11–14); Tertullian of Carthage, the first great Christian writer in Latin (**16.7** – 16.15); the Egyptian gnostic, Theodotus (**16.8** – 16.16); and Origen, who succeeded Clement as head of the school at Alexandria (**16.9** – 16.17–20).

The third and fourth centuries produced the *Apostolic Church Order* (**16.10** – 16.21), a religious romance known as the *Clementine Homilies* (**16.11** – 16.22, 23), and two Syrian books – one of sermons entitled the *Book of Stages* (**16.12** – 16.24–32) and the other containing church law and known as the *Apostolic Constitutions* (**16.13** – 16.33, 34).

2 *First Clement* (late first century)

This letter was written about AD 96 by the church in Rome to the church in Corinth to deal with fierce strife there caused by the deposition of certain elders. It has been ascribed to Clement, third or fourth Bishop of Rome, traditionally identified with the Clement mentioned in Philippians 4.3 as being one of Paul's fellow workers.

16.1 – 13.1 *and 2*   A

. . . especially remembering the words of the Lord Jesus
which he spoke while teaching
about gentleness and patience.
For he spoke thus:
'Be merciful that you may obtain mercy.
Forgive that you may be forgiven.
As you do, so will it be done to you.
As you give, so will it be given to you.
As you judge, so will you be judged.
As you are kind, so will kindness be shown to you.
With what measure you measure,
it will be measured to you.'

These words of Jesus are quoted in order to encourage Corinthian Christians to be humble and not arrogant or conceited or boastful. They are reminiscent of sayings of Jesus in the Sermon on the Mount (Matthew 5.7; 6.14; 7.1f., 12).

---

3 Second Clement (mid-second century)

A sermon rather than a letter, this document was not composed by the author of *First Clement*. Its origin, recipient and date are all uncertain but it is usually thought to belong to the mid-second century. It sets out the character of the Christian life and the duty of repentance.

16.2 – 4.2   B

Not everyone who says to me, Lord, Lord,
will be saved
but he who does righteousness.

In Matthew 7.21, being saved is interpreted as entering the kingdom and righteousness is identified with doing the will of the Father.

16.3 – 4.5   c

If you are gathered together with me in my bosom
and do not my commandments
I will cast you away and say to you,
'Depart from me,
I do not know from where you came,
you workers of iniquity.'

Similarly, in the parable of the sheep and the goats, Jesus dismisses those who failed to help the needy, 'Depart from me, you cursed' (Matthew 25.41).

16.4 – 5.2–4   b

'You will be as lambs in the midst of wolves.'
Peter said: 'What if the wolves tear the lambs?'
Jesus said:
'Let not the lambs after their death fear the wolves.
So you also fear not those who kill you
and are unable to do anything to you;
but fear him who after your death
has power over soul and body
to cast them into the valley of fire.'

According to Matthew 10.16, Jesus warned his disciples that they were being sent out as sheep (lambs in Luke 10.3) in the midst of wolves. Here he tells them that they are not to fear the wolves but God, who, according to Matthew 10.28, 'can destroy both soul and body in Gehenna' – a valley to the south of Jerusalem where, according to popular Jewish belief, the last judgement was to take place. In the gospels, it is the place of punishment in the next life.

165

16.5 – 8.5f.   B

**If you did not guard what is small
who shall give you what is great?
For I say to you:
he who is faithful in what is least
is faithful also in what is much.**

In the parable of the talents, the master praises the first two servants for being faithful over a little and proceeds to set them over much (Matthew 25.21, 23). The author of *Second Clement* interprets this as a requirement to keep the flesh pure and the seal (of baptism) undefiled so that we may obtain eternal life.

16.6 – 9.11   A

**My brothers are those who do
the will of my Father.**

In Matthew 12.50, the person who does the Father's will is brother, sister and mother of Jesus, as in the *Gospel of the Ebionites* (15.8).

16.7 – 12.2   D

**When the two will be one
and the outside as the inside
and the male with the female
neither male nor female.**

This is said to be the reply of Jesus to someone who asked when his kingdom would come. There is a longer form in *Thomas* 22b (10.26).

4 Justin Martyr (about AD 100 to about AD 165)

Born of pagan parents in Samaria, Justin searched after the truth in pagan philosophies but finally accepted Christianity about

AD 130. While teaching at Ephesus, he engaged in a long argument with a liberal-minded Jew named Trypho. He moved to Rome, where he opened a Christian school. Tatian (**8.13**) was one of his pupils. The first Christian writer to attempt to reconcile the claims of faith and reason, Justin wrote two books in defence of Christianity, the first addressed to the Emperor, the second to the Roman Senate. Eventually, he and some of his disciples were denounced to the authorities as Christians. Having refused to recant, they were scourged and beheaded. The following sayings are from his *Dialogue with Trypho*.

16.8 – Dialogue 35.3   A

There will be dissensions and squabbles.

Before quoting this saying, Justin refers to the coming of false prophets (Matthew 7.15) and false Messiahs (Matthew 24.5) who would deceive many. Such people will cause divisions within the Christian community.[1] There is a similar warning about divisions even within families in Matthew 10.34–36; Luke 12.49–53; *Thomas* 16 (11.11).

16.9 – Dialogue 47.5   A

In whatever situations I find you I shall judge you.

Although several writers quote these words, only Justin expressly attributes them to Jesus. The warning to be prepared for the day of judgement is found in several places in the New Testament, including parables such as those of the servants waiting for their master to return at an unknown hour (Luke 12.35–38), a householder not knowing when the thief might break in (Matthew 24.43; Luke 12.39; *Thomas* 103 – 9.27), and the foolish bridesmaids who were unprepared for the bridegroom's arrival (Matthew 25.1–13).[2]

---

5 Irenaeus (about AD 130 to about AD 200)

Irenaeus was Bishop of Lyons from about AD 178 (**1.7**). His principal work was *Against all Heresies* – an attack especially upon gnosticism (**1.4**).

16.10 – 5.33.3 c

The days will come in which vines will spring up,
each having ten thousand stalks,
and on each stalk ten thousand branches. . . .
Likewise a grain of wheat will engender
ten thousand ears of corn
and each ear will hold ten thousand grains. . . .
And all animals using these foods . . .
will live in peace and concord,
subject to man with all subjection.

Irenaeus is quoting from Papias (about AD 60 to 130), Bishop of Hierapolis in Asia Minor, who is quoting from the elders who had heard the Apostle John telling about this discourse of Jesus in which he foretells abundant fruitfulness and peace on earth.

---

6 Clement of Alexandria (about AD 150 to about AD 215)

Clement was head of the famous catechetical school at Alexandria for thirteen or fourteen years. One of the three of his greatest works to survive is called *Stromateis* or *Miscellanies*. In this, he deals with the relationship between faith and knowledge. He quotes sayings of Jesus from the lost *Gospel of the Hebrews* (**15.4**) and *Gospel of the Egyptians* (**15.5**) and also a few others.

In *Miscellanies* 2.9.45, he quotes from the *Gospel of the Hebrews* the saying of Jesus about wondering, reigning and resting (15.11). Later (5.14.96), he gives a longer version without saying where he found it (15.12). This longer version appears also in Oxyrhynchus Papyrus 654 in fragmentary form as the second of six sayings of Jesus (6.10).

In *Miscellanies* 3.45 (15.16) and 3.63 (15.17), Clement quotes from the *Gospel of the Egyptians* in order to refute those who object to marriage.

Four sayings with biblical echoes follow (16.11–14).

16.11 – Miscellanies 1.24.158 A

Ask for the big things and the little things will be added to you.

Compare Matthew 6.33; Luke 12.31 (Q) – 'Seek first his kingdom and all these things will be added to you.' The same principle is applied here to prayer. Origen quotes a longer version (16.18).[3]

16.12 – Miscellanies 1.28.177 A

Become skilled money-changers, rejecting some but retaining the good.

This saying occurs more often than any other in early Christian writings.[4] Origen (**16.9**) quotes it in his *Commentary on John* and it is found three times in the *Clementine Homilies* (**16.11**). Sometimes the words are applied to the ability to discern between genuine sayings of Jesus and spurious ones (**3.11**). The saying is also used with regard to 'books written to try us' – presumably a reference to the sifting of books during the second period of the growth of the canon of the New Testament (**1.8**). It is possible that they may lie behind Paul's advice in 1 Thessalonians 5.21f. – 'Test everything, hold on to the good, abstain from every form of evil.' The last words have been taken as being a reference to counterfeit coinage. This is borne out by the extended quotation found here in the *Clementine Homilies* – 'rejecting some but retaining the good'. Pilgrims attending one of the festivals in the Temple at Jerusalem required to change their currency. When they offered a coin to a money-changer sitting at his counter he would test it by letting it fall on his table or by weighing it in his scales. The sound it made or its weight would indicate whether it was good or bad. A skilled money-changer would retain the good but reject the counterfeit.[5]

16.13 – Miscellanies 2.9.45.4   B

Wonder at the things before you.

Clement quotes this as coming from the *Traditions of Matthias* and compares it with a saying of the Greek philosopher, Plato: 'This is the mark of a philosopher, wondering; for there is no other beginning of philosophy than this' (*Theaetetus* 155D). He interprets both as implying that wonder is the first step towards knowledge of things beyond and quotes from the *Gospel of the Hebrews* about wonder leading to reigning and then to rest (15.11). Compare *Thomas* 2 (10.2).

Whether or not this saying is authentic, it is certainly true in all realms of knowledge that the sense of wonder leads to discovery: for example, Archimedes and the law of specific gravity, James Watt and the invention of the steam engine. It is no less the case in the spiritual realm. We are reminded in Acts 7.31 that it was amazement at the sight of the bush that burned without being consumed that led to God's revelation of his name to Moses.

16.14 – Miscellanies 5.10.63   C

The Lord said in a certain gospel: 'My mystery is for me and the sons of my house.'

While the majority of people did not fully understand the message of the parables of Jesus, it was granted to his disciples to know the mysteries of the kingdom of God (Matthew 13.11; Mark 4.11; Luke 8.10; *Thomas* 62 – 12.25). For Christians, God's secret plans kept hidden from the creation of the world have now been revealed in Jesus Christ and his gospel.

---

7 Tertullian (about AD 160 to 225)

Tertullian was brought up in Carthage as a pagan but became
the first great Christian writer in Latin. He was the author of
many books in defence of Christianity.

16.15 – Concerning Baptism B

No one can obtain the kingdom of heaven who has not passed through temptation.

Tertullian tells us exactly where he found this saying in the
gospel, just before Jesus said to his disciples in the Garden of
Gethsemane: 'Watch and pray that you may not enter into
temptation' (Mark 14.38). Although Jesus encouraged his
disciples to pray that they should not be led into temptation
(Matthew 6.13), he realized that temptation was inevitable and
stressed the necessity of overcoming it.

---

8 Theodotus (second-century Egyptian gnostic)

16.16 c

Save yourself and your life.

In Genesis 19.17, we read that Lot was told to flee for his life
from the wicked city of Sodom. Jesus alluded to this incident in
prophesying about the future coming of the Son of man (Luke
17.28–32). Then he proceeded to declare that, in order to gain
one's life, one had to lose it and that whoever loses his life will
save it (Luke 17.33).

---

9 Origen (about AD 185 to about AD 254)

Origen (**1.8**) was the favourite pupil of Clement of Alexandria
(**16.6**) and one of the greatest teachers in the early Church.
When Clement was forced to withdraw from the catechetical
school on account of persecution, Origen took over, though only

eighteen years old. Later, he founded a school at Caesarea. He died from torture in the persecution of Decius at the age of sixty-nine.

16.17 – Commentary on Matthew   c

Because of the weak I was weak;
because of the hungry I was hungry;
because of the thirsty I was thirsty.

At first sight, this looks like an adaptation of words in the parable of the sheep and the goats – 'I was hungry and you fed me; I was thirsty and you gave me drink; I was sick and you visited me' (Matthew 25.35f.); but perhaps it should be looked upon rather as an expansion of the words of Isaiah regarding the suffering servant who bore our griefs and carried our sorrows (Isaiah 53.4) quoted in Matthew 8.17.

16.18 – Selections on the Psalms   A

This is what you must do:
Ask for the big things
and the little things will be added to you;
ask for the heavenly things
and the earthly things will be added to you.

There is a shorter version of this saying in Clement of Alexandria (16.11). This expansion brings the saying even more into line with the teaching of Jesus in the Lord's Prayer. There he taught his disciples to pray for heavenly things – the hallowing of God's name, the coming of God's kingdom, the doing of God's will – before earthly things – daily bread, forgiveness, protection.

16.19 – Homily on Jeremiah   c

Sodom is justified more than you.

These words are said to be part of the reproach of Jesus to Jerusalem. They could be derived from Ezekiel's comparison of its inhabitants with those of Sodom: 'Because of your sins they are more in the right than you' (Ezekiel 16.52). They also recall the lament of Jesus over Jerusalem for killing the prophets and stoning those sent to it (Matthew 23.37; Luke 13.34). The point would seem to be that the sins of Jerusalem were worse than those of Sodom. The people of Jerusalem were being given a chance that those of Sodom were not given – the opportunity of accepting or rejecting the Messiah.

16.20 – Homily on Jeremiah   A

He who is near me is near the fire,
but he who is far from me
is far from the kingdom.

This warning about persecution occurs also in *Thomas* 82 (12.33) and is similar to many in the canonical gospels. It is linked here with the thought that to run away from it is to miss the joy of God's kingdom. The antithesis of far and near appears also in Oxyrhynchus Papyrus 1224 (6.21). Origen cannot remember where he read this saying, but it looks as if he considered it authentic. His source was probably the *Gospel of Thomas*.

10 The *Apostolic Church Order* (third century)

This early Christian document contains regulations on church practice and moral discipline. Its contents are attributed to various apostles, who are alleged to have met at a council at which Mary and Martha were also present. It is thought to have been composed sometime during the third century.

16.21   c

The weak will be saved through the strong

The context of this saying[6] is a discussion on the ministry of women. Should they be present at the celebration of the Lord's Supper? They were not with the disciples when Jesus had said, 'This is my body and blood'. Martha declared that the reason for this was that Jesus had seen Mary smiling. Mary replied that she had not laughed but that Jesus had previously made this statement in the course of his teaching. It would seem that the reference is to the person who is weak in faith, or perhaps even without faith, being saved by his wife or her husband who is strong in faith, as Paul suggests in 1 Corinthians 7.16.

11 The *Clementine Homilies* (third or fourth century)

This religious romance arranged in the form of twenty discourses sent from Rome to James the Just in Jerusalem under the name of Clement of Rome (first century) dates from the third or fourth century. It contains several quotations from the gospels and a few other sayings of Jesus, including the following.

16.22 – 2.51; 3.50; 18.20 A

Become skilled money-changers.

In the second and third discourses, we are told that Jesus said this because there are genuine and spurious words (see 16.23). In the eighteenth discourse, the saying is used with reference to 'books written to try us' – presumably a reference to the sifting of books during the second period of the growth of the canon of the New Testament (**1.8**). Clement of Alexandria (**16.12**) and Origen (**16.9**) are two other early Christian writers who quote this saying.

16.23 – 3.50 A

Why do you not perceive that which is reasonable in the scriptures?

Sound judgement between genuine and spurious sayings is said to be the meaning of these words of Jesus in Matthew 22.29 (compare 16.22).

---

12 The *Book of Stages* (fourth century)

The anonymous author of this Syrian work describes in thirty sermons or discourses the stages by means of which people can reach perfection in this world – humility towards all, poverty, and chastity of heart and body. The following are selected from many sayings attributed to Jesus in these sermons – sayings that illustrate the ascetic way of life characteristic of early Syriac Christianity (**8.14**).[7]

16.24 – *Sermon 2.2.10*   B

I did not come to judge the world
but to teach them in humility
and to save them
and to become an example to my disciples
so that they might do as I do.

In John 3.17, we are told that God sent his Son into the world to save rather than to condemn. In the upper room, Jesus washed the feet of his disciples as an example 'that you should do as I have done to you' (John 13.15).

16.25 – *Sermon 2.6.2*   C

Everyone who does not walk in my footsteps
and does not go into the houses of tax-collectors
and prostitutes and teach them
as I have shown him
will not be perfect.

Jesus was criticized for being the friend of tax collectors and sinners (Matthew 11.19) and for eating with them (Mark 2.16; Luke 19.7). Jesus justified his actions by comparing himself with a doctor who treats those who are ill (Matthew 9.12; Mark 2.17; Luke 5.31). Yet, according to another Arabic saying (17.22), he realized the dangers his followers could be in by following his example.

16.26 – Sermon 3.3   B

As you are found
you will be taken up.

There is a similar saying in Justin's *Dialogue with Trypho* (16.9), where it is linked with the idea of judgement: 'I will judge you.'[8] Here in 16.26 the passive is found, 'You will be taken up', perhaps to avoid using God's name – the reverential passive.

16.27 – Sermon 3.6   C

Anyone who possesses anything
is not worthy of me.

In Luke 14.33, such renunciation is demanded of those who wish to be disciples of Jesus: 'Everyone of you who does not keep on saying good-bye to everything that he has cannot be my disciple.' The present tense of the verb in Luke indicates a continual readiness to give up all one's possessions in order to follow Jesus.[9]

16.28 – Sermon 5.18   C

The world is incapable of the Paraclete
but the children of the age who are just
are capable of the gifts of union.

Union with the Holy Spirit seems to be what is being referred to here as the preserve of those who act according to the law.

16.29 – Sermon 9.12   c

I will give you the perfection
which I will accomplish when I come.
When I send the Paraclete
I will make you perfect
because you wait for me
and strive for the perfection of the angels above
from which your father Adam fell.
I will take you and your father Adam
up to the height from which you have fallen.

In the farewell discourse in chapters 14 to 16 of John's Gospel, Jesus promised to send the Holy Spirit as a perpetual presence (John 14.15–17), a perpetual teacher (John 14.25f.), a perpetual witness to himself (John 15.26f.), a perpetual convictor of wrong (John 16.7–11) and as a perpetual revealer of the truth (John 16.12–15). Here, the purpose of the coming of the Holy Spirit is said to be the restoration of the perfection which Adam had before the fall.

16.30 – Sermon 25.4   c

Be humble and separated and sanctified
from the world and from marriage
and love all people and follow me.
Refuse to be of the world
as I was not of it nor have I worked in it;
but follow me and be perfect.

In Matthew 5.48, the perfection characteristic of God and expected of the followers of Jesus includes love for enemies as well as for friends (Matthew 5.44). Here it comprises in addition humility, separation from the world, and celibacy, all of which were characteristic of the early Syrian Church.

16.31 – Sermon 29.8 A

Be untiring in prayer.

The parable of the unjust judge who granted the request of a widow who pestered him (Luke 18.2–5) was told by Jesus to stress that we ought always to pray and not lose heart (Luke 18.1). Paul may have been quoting this saying of Jesus when he told the Christians at Thessalonica to pray constantly (1 Thessalonians 5.17). On the other hand, it is possible that this is an example of what Jeremias sees as the frequent practice in the *Book of Stages* of quoting a Pauline text as a saying of the Lord.[10]

16.32 – Sermon 30.11 C

Do not throw what is holy to the dogs
nor pearls to pigs
lest they trample them with their feet
and turn and break you away from your doctrine.

The unexpected twist at the end of this saying makes it different from the warning in Matthew 7.6. There it is said that the pigs may turn and attack the people throwing the pearls, whereas here the reference to doctrine indicates a later interpretation.

---

13 The *Apostolic Constitutions* (fourth century)

This collection of church law dating from the latter half of the fourth century is thought to have originated in Syria. It contains many quotations from the four gospels, some of which are explicitly stated to have been sayings of Jesus. Only those that have significant differences from the New Testament are given here.

16.33 – 2.60 B

How can such an one even now avoid hearing
that word of the Lord,
'The Gentiles are justified more than you'?

**as he says, by way of reproach to Jerusalem,
'Sodom is justified rather than you.'**

'Such an one' is the person who takes pains about temporary
things night and day but does not take care of things that endure
for ever. The first saying may be a quotation from Ezekiel 16.52,
where Jerusalem is upbraided for unfaithfulness. Sodom and
Samaria 'are more in the right than you'. It is possible that the
second saying also is being attributed here to God and not to
Jesus, though Origen attributes the words to Jesus (16.19). Jesus
did compare those who rejected him with the people of Sodom. If
the mighty works done in Capernaum had been done in Sodom,
its inhabitants would not have been destroyed (Matthew 11.23).

16.34 – 8.12 B

**Drink this, all of you;
for this is my blood poured out for many
for the forgiveness of sins.
Keep on doing this in my remembrance.
For as often as you eat this bread
and drink this cup
you proclaim my death until I come.**

The first part of this saying over the cup is close to Matthew
26.28. The command to repeat the act with reference to the cup
is found in 1 Corinthians 11.25 (4.3). The words of interpretation in the third person – '. . . you proclaim the death of
the Lord until he comes' – are added by Paul to the words of
institution (1 Corinthians 11.26). In the *Apostolic Constitutions*,
they are put into the mouth of Jesus himself. In addition, the
Liturgy of St Mark (fourth or fifth century) completes the saying
over the cup as follows: '. . . you proclaim my death and confess
my resurrection and ascension, until I come.'

179

CHAPTER SEVENTEEN

Arabic Gems

1 Christianity and Islam

In this chapter, we shall be searching for Arabic gems in various Moslem writings. Since Islam was not founded until the seventh century AD, it is unlikely that much authentic tradition about Jesus, independent of the New Testament, will be found in its sacred books, chief of which is the Koran. Nevertheless, as Christianity spread in the early centuries, missionaries moved east and south as well as north and west, in obedience to the command of Jesus to go into all the world teaching all nations (Matthew 28.18–20). They would have taken some good and ancient traditions with them to out-of-the-way corners of Arabia and Mesopotamia. It is possible that this involved the handing on by word of mouth of some otherwise unrecorded sayings of Jesus.

In addition, Mohammed (AD 570–632) knew Jews and Christians. He had discussions about religion with one of his first wife's cousins who was a Christian with some knowledge of the Bible. It is also likely that other Moslem contacts with Christians resulted in oral tradition being transmitted through Arabic authors.

2 Jesus in Islam

For Mohammed and for Moslems in general Jesus was one of the prophets, whose message was brought to completion by the revelations made to Mohammed. While he deplored the Jewish refusal to recognize Jesus as a teacher sent from God, Mohammed also deplored the ascription to him of divine honours by

Christians. To him, this undermined the indisputable doctrine of monotheism, enshrined in the Islamic motto: 'There is no God but Allah and Mohammed is the prophet of Allah.' As far as Islam is concerned, Jesus is a servant of God and even a prophet, but not Son of God.

3 Jesus in the Koran

In the Koran, Jesus is regularly referred to as son of Mary – *'Isa ibn Maryam*. On account of its late date as compared with the New Testament, it is unlikely that much, if any, new authentic material about Jesus can be found in it. Of the several sayings attributed to him in the Koran, only two or three give any semblance of authenticity.[1]

17.1 – *Koran 3.44f.*   c

'Fear God and obey me.
Allah is my God and your God.
So serve him.
That is the straight path.'
When Jesus perceived their unbelief, he said:
'Who will be my helpers in the cause of God?'
The disciples replied:
'We will be God's helpers.
We believe in God.
Bear witness
that we have surrendered ourselves to him.'

Apart from the reference to Allah, there is nothing in these words that could not have been said by Jesus or his disciples. According to Roderic Dunkerley, ' "Fear God and obey me" crystallizes the teaching of many passages and is in itself a fine precept.'[2]

17.2 – Koran 5.76 c

O children of Israel, worship God, my Lord and your Lord.

Like Judaism and Christianity, Islam believes that there is only one God, whom Moslems call Allah (**17.2**). While they worship God as Lord, they refuse to say of Jesus, as Thomas said after the resurrection, 'My Lord and my God' (John 20.28).

17.3 – Koran 43.63–64 d

I have come to you with wisdom and that I may make clear to you some of that whereon you are at variance. So fear God and obey me. Assuredly Allah is my God and your God. So serve him. This is the straight path.

'Fear God and obey me' and 'Serve God', repeated from an earlier chapter in the Koran (17.1), are suitable commands for Christians.

17.4 – Koran 61.6 d

Children of Israel, I am indeed God's apostle to you confirming the law which was given before me and to announce an apostle that shall come after me whose name shall be Ahmed.

This alleged saying is intended to show that Jesus had foretold the coming of Mohammed. As proof of this, the Persian paraphrase of the Koran quotes the promise of Jesus to send the *Parakletos* ('Comforter') to the disciples (John 16.7). This is confused with *periklutos* ('famous'), which has the same meaning as Ahmed, one of the names of Mohammed. Both Ahmed and Mohammed come from the same root and have approximately the same significance.

17.5 – Koran 61.14   D

Believers, be God's helpers
as Jesus son of Mary said to the apostles:
'Who will be my helpers?'
The apostles said: 'We will be God's helpers.'

Jesus' command to be God's helpers is repeated here from chapter 3 in the Koran (17.1).

---

4 Outside the Koran

Many sayings attributed to Jesus have been discovered in Arabic literature outside the Koran. In 1893, D. S. Margoliouth, Professor of Arabic at Oxford, published 77 Arabic sayings in the *Expository Times*.[3]

In an article published in 1904,[4] J. H. Ropes included 51 Arabic sayings along with 66 from various other sources, a total of 117. While he regarded only 10 of the 66 as seeming with considerable probability to possess historical value, he declared that the unwritten sayings from Islamic sources were chiefly of merely curious interest.

The largest collection of these was made by a Spanish scholar, Professor Michael Asin of Madrid. In 1919 and 1925, he published 233 Arabic sayings.[5] Of these, 225 were given in Arabic with a Latin translation, while the remainder were in Latin or French. Not all were sayings attributed to Jesus, however. Michael Asin was convinced that many of the sayings he collected were genuine, his favourite phrase being: 'This seems to me to be an unwritten saying.'

In 1929, James Robson, Professor of Arabic at Manchester University, made a comprehensive collection of the Arabic sayings of Christ in Islam.[6] He came to the conclusion that, while in many cases one need have no hesitation in denying the genuineness of passages, in others there may be a possibility of authenticity; but there must always be a doubt.

5 Beyond the Gospels

Like Michael Asin and James Robson, Roderic Dunkerley felt that some of the Arabic sayings were genuine.[7] It was not unlikely that unrecorded sayings were cherished in out-of-the-way parts of Arabia and Mesopotamia. He was prepared to consider favourably sayings whose ascription was definite, unchallenged, early and attested by several witnesses. This was especially true if a particular saying contained teaching that was opposed to Islam yet was preserved in Moslem tradition. His final criterion was aptness and precision similar to those in sayings of Jesus in the canonical gospels.

Using these criteria, Roderic Dunkerley considered that many could be rejected outright. There is a large number of ascetic passages, for example. This phenomenon ties in with the great emphasis on asceticism in the Nestorian Church, which flourished in Mesopotamia from the fifth century, especially in Edessa (**8.10; 8.14**), and with the presence of many Christian monks in that area. Even though there are many ascetic sayings in the New Testament, many of this group must belong to an age when asceticism was thought to be necessary for salvation and not to the time of Jesus. Asceticism is not characteristic of the Koran, but was imported into orthodox Islam from Arabian monasticism, chiefly through the work of al-Ghazzali in the eleventh and twelfth centuries (**17.6**).

The conclusion seems to be that Arabic sayings attributed to Jesus are, for the most part, of doubtful authenticity (C or D), but there are a few gems which could be genuine (B).[8] For this chapter, I have selected those that can be classified as B or C. I have included a few of more doubtful authenticity (D) on account of their vivid or colourful character.

6 al-Ghazzali

Most of the sayings published by Michael Asin in his first collection in 1919 were from the great homiletic encyclopaedia by al-Ghazzali (AD 1058–1111) known as the *Revival of the Religious Sciences.*

Abu Hamid Muhammed al-Ghazzali was one of the most famous figures in Islam. He wrote about seventy books, of which this encyclopaedia was his greatest. He was recognized as being the greatest contemporary authority on Islamic theology and law and one of the finest mystical writers. He reformed the ascetic movement known as Sufism, from the garments of coarse wool (*suf*) worn by ascetics, and made it an integral part of orthodox Islam (**17.5**).

Although al-Ghazzali lived in the eleventh and twelfth centuries, some of the sayings and other traditions quoted by him go back several centuries, if not to the first centuries of the Christian era at least to the seventh century. Occasionally, sayings of Jesus are attributed to Mohammed.

17.6 – 1.24.5 [Asin 2]   c

How many trees there are!
but not all bear fruit.
How many fruits there are!
but not all are good.
How many sciences there are!
but not all are useful.

Variety of knowledge is added here to the idea of trees being known by their fruits in Matthew 7.16–20; 12.33; Luke 6.43–45. In Luke 13.6–9, there is the parable of the fig tree which was not bearing fruit.

17.7 – 1.27.4 [Asin 3]   c

Commit not wisdom to those
who are not meet for it
lest you harm it;
and withhold it not from those
who are meet for it
lest you harm them.

Be like a good doctor
who applies medication to the wound.

Both this and the following saying recommend discrimination in the preaching and teaching of the gospel message. Only those who are ready for it should be told the secret of the kingdom of God, a principle which Jesus followed in his own ministry (Mark 4.11). Yet he himself was ready, like a good doctor, to go where he was most needed (Luke 19.10).

17.8 – 1.43.4 [Asin 4]   c

Do not hang pearls on the necks of pigs;
for wisdom is better than pearls
and whoever despises it is worse than pigs.

This is very similar to the warning in Matthew 7.6 and *Thomas* 93 (12.28) not to throw pearls before pigs, though the reference to wisdom recalls Proverbs 3.15, where wisdom is said to be more precious than jewels. Proverbs 11.22 likens a beautiful woman without discretion to a gold ring in a pig's snout.

17.9 – 1.45.14 [Asin 5]   c

Evil scholars are like a rock
fallen at the mouth of a brook.
It neither drinks the water
nor lets it flow to the fields.
They are like a drain pipe
plastered outside and foul inside.
They are like decorated graves
full of dead men's bones.

Similarly, Jesus denounced scribes and Pharisees who shut the kingdom of heaven to other people and remained outside themselves (Matthew 23.13). They were like whitewashed tombs (Matthew 23.27).

17.10 – 2.124.1 [Asin 16]   c

'What would you do if you
saw your brother sleeping
and the wind had lifted his garment?'
His disciples said: 'We would cover him up.'
He said: 'No; you would uncover him.'
They said: 'God forbid! Who would do this?'
He said: 'One of you who hears
a word concerning his brother
and adds to it and relates it with additions.'

This is an effective warning against gossiping and tale-bearing. In the Sermon on the Mount, there is a section on oaths (Matthew 5.33–37), in which pure truthfulness is recommended: 'Let your word be "Yes!" or "No!". Anything beyond these comes from the evil one.' Similarly, gossiping would be forbidden by the golden rule given by Jesus: 'All things that you wish people to do to you do also to them' (Matthew 7.12). In line with the teaching of Jesus, James warns about the tongue being as a fire that needs to be kept under control (James 1.26; 3.6) and about not disparaging a brother (James 4.11). In *The Parables of Jesus*, A. T. Cadoux declares that the Arabic tale 'has every internal mark of genuineness' while Roderic Dunkerley describes it as 'an interesting and telling little story – none of us thinks he gossips! The illustration is very clever – "sleeping" suggests the ignorance of the man regarding what people are saying; the wind typifies the uncertain and often quite innocent origin of these unhappy murmurs; while the deliberate uncovering aptly represents the careless and unkindly development of the tale. It might well enshrine an actual reminiscence.'[9]

17.11 – 3.80.6 [Asin 25]   c

Jesus was asked guidance about entering Paradise.
He said: 'Do not ever speak.'
His disciples said: 'We cannot do that.'
He said: 'Then never speak anything but good.'

When someone asked Jesus what he should do to inherit eternal life, Jesus quoted some of the commandments (Matthew 19.16–19; Mark 10.17–19; Luke 18.18–20). Here, a similar question evokes a warning about careless talk such as occurs in Matthew 12.34–37 or in James 1.26 (see 17.10).

17.12 – 3.81.4 [Asin 26]   D

Devotion comprises ten parts.
Nine of them consist in silence
and one in solitude.

Though solitude is an aid to devotion, even more important, according to this alleged saying, is the attitude of waiting upon God in silence. This goes even further than the command to pray to the Father in secret found in Matthew 6.6.

17.13 – 3.100.9 [Asin 29]   C

The apostles said:
'How foul is the smell of this dog!'
Jesus said: 'How white are its teeth!'

These were the differing reactions to the sight and smell of a dead dog seen by Jesus and his disciples.[10] According to another version of this story, Jesus said:

How lovely are its teeth,
so sharp, and white as pearls.

A twelfth-century Persian poet, Nizami, wrote a poem on this incident. One English version of it is contained in a book of lyrics by Ellice Hopkins.[11] It tells how, after one had spurned 'the gaunt-ribbed carcase of a homeless dog' and another had complained that, 'living or dead, he smells not of the rose', from the crowd a mild voice cries,

No pearl the whiteness of his teeth outvies.

Then all men in their spirit knew, who heard,
Jesus of Nazareth's must be that word.
For only he had love's divinity,
Even in a dead dog some good to see.

17.14 – 3.140.10 [Asin 35]   c

The love of this world and of the next
cannot coexist in a believer's heart
even as fire and water
cannot remain in a single vessel.

This echoes the warning given by Jesus in Matthew 6.24 and Luke 16.13 about the impossibility of being a slave to two masters at one and the same time. There is also an Arabic saying about the impossibility of pleasing two wives (17.28).

17.15 – 3.149.5 [Asin 48]   c

Whoever craves wealth
is like a man who drinks sea water;
the more he drinks,
the more he increases his thirst,
and he ceases not to drink
until he perishes.

This is one of the very few sayings of Jesus found in the collection of Persian proverbs by a Christian writer, Levinus Warnerus, in 1644. It is a striking warning of the danger of seeking to amass wealth – the more one gets the more one wants.

17.16 – 3.182.18 [Asin 53]   d

What benefit is it to a dark house
to have a lamp on its roof
when all is dark within?

> *Even so it is no benefit to you*
> *to have the light of knowledge*
> *upon your lips and not in your hearts.*

In the Sermon on the Mount, there is the parable of the lamp which gives light to all in the house (Matthew 5.15; compare Mark 4.21; Luke 8.16). Here the lamp is on the roof and all is dark within. This stress on the necessity of integrity and purity within is a lesson taught elsewhere; for example, in the prohibition of lustful thoughts (Matthew 5.28) and in the denunciation of the hypocrisy of scribes and Pharisees who are like whitewashed tombs, outwardly beautiful but inwardly unclean (Matthew 23.27).

17.17 – 3.247.14 [Asin 60]   D

Splendid dress, proud heart.

This recalls the words of Jesus in Mark 12.38 about the scribes who like to walk around in long robes while they receive salutations in the market place.

17.18 – 4.164.14 [Asin 80]   D

> *I commend to you pure water,*
> *wild herbs and barley bread.*
> *Beware of wheaten bread,*
> *for which you cannot give*
> *worthy thanks to God.*

The contrast here is between the simple fare of ordinary people and the more sumptuous food of the rich. Five barley loaves and two small fish were the contents of the picnic basket of the lad who helped Jesus at the feeding of the large crowd of people according to John 6.9. In the synoptic gospels, the lad is not mentioned and the food is described as five loaves and two fish without any reference to the make-up of the loaves or the size of the fish (Matthew 14.17; Mark 6.38; Luke 9.13). It is not altogether clear why, according to this Arabic saying, one cannot give worthy thanks to God for wheaten bread.

17.19 – 4.190.14 [Asin 82]   B

Look at the birds:
they do not sow
or reap or gather into barns
and God sustains them from day to day.
If however you say:
but we are endowed with a larger stomach,
then I say to you:
Look at the camels
how God has created sustenance for them.

This is an interesting expansion of the saying in Matthew 6.26: 'Look at the birds of the air for they do not sow or reap or gather into barns, and your heavenly Father feeds them.' In another Arabic saying (17.26), little ants and wild beasts occur in place of camels.

---

7 Other Sources

17.20 – *Jacut*, Geographical Lexicon
[Margoliouth 2]   C

The world is a place of transition,
full of examples.
Be pilgrims in it
and take warning
by the traces of those who have gone before.

The roll-call of the faithful in Hebrews 11 comes to a climax in Hebrews 12.1 with the exhortation to lay aside every sin since we are surrounded by so great a cloud of witnesses. Compare also the Arabic bridge saying (17.30). It is interesting that this saying about the transitoriness of this world is quoted in a geographical lexicon.

17.21 – *Baidawi*, Commentary on the Koran
[Margoliouth 3] B

Be in the midst, yet walk on one side.

This is very similar to the prayer of Jesus in John 17.11 and 16 that his disciples should be in the world but not of it. However, Margoliouth points out that the context indicates that it has to do with avowing friendship while concealing enmity. It is possible that the original meaning has been distorted by its context.

17.22 – *Zamakhshari*, Commentary on the Koran
[Margoliouth 41] D

Beware how you sit with sinners.

This is said to have been written in the sermons of Jesus, as if Jesus wrote sermons. In Mark 2.16, we read that he himself was criticized by Pharisees for doing exactly this – eating with tax collectors and sinners.

17.23 – *Ibn 'Abd Rabbihi [Asin 117]* C
(*tenth century*)

The world is a field belonging to the devil and worldly people are its farmers.

Some of the phrases here are reminiscent of the parable of the weeds in Matthew 13.36–43 – 'the field is the world', 'the enemy is the devil', 'the weeds are the sons of the evil one'.

17.24 – Ibn 'Abd Rabbihi [Asin 118] c
(tenth century)

**I am he who turned the world over on its face
for I have neither a wife who can die
nor a house which can be destroyed.**

In John 16.33, Jesus declares that he has overcome the world. Here he has turned things upside down by leading an ascetic life without a house in which to shelter – as in Matthew 8.20; Luke 9.58; *Thomas* 86 (11.8).

17.25 – Samarqandi, Awakening of the Negligent *156.2*
(tenth century)
[Asin 144] c

**What benefit is it to a blind man
to carry a lamp to illuminate others
but not himself?
What benefit is it to a dark house
if a lamp is placed on its roof?
What benefit is it to you if you speak wisely
but act foolishly?**

For the picture of a lamp on the roof of a dark house, see 17.16. There the moral is the importance of inner purity as well as wise words; here it is the necessity of actions matching up to one's speech.

17.26 – Samarqandi 168.9 [Asin 146] c

**Do not preserve food for tomorrow
for tomorrow will come
and with it food necessary for your life.
Look at the little ant and who sustains it.
If you say that
the stomachs of little ants are small
look at the bird.**

> *But if you say the bird has wings*
> *look at the wild beasts,*
> *how large and fat are their bodies!*

In the account of the provision of manna in the desert for the Israelites, Moses told the people not to keep any of it for the following day (Exodus 16.19). Yet it is possible that in the Lord's Prayer Jesus taught his disciples to pray for the provision today of bread for the following day (see 15.2). In Matthew 6.25–27 and Luke 12.22–24, it is anxious worrying about food that was condemned by Jesus. In addition to the birds found in Matthew 6.26 and Luke 12.24 as illustrations of trustful dependence on God's provision, ants and wild beasts are included here. In 17.19, camels take the place of wild beasts. In Proverbs 30.25, ants are one of four species of animals commended for their wisdom. Weak though they are, they store up food for themselves in the summer.

17.27 – Samarqandi 220.11 [Asin 150]   D

> *It is by no means amazing how anyone perishes;*
> *but it is amazing how anyone is saved.*

After his conversion, John Newton (1725–1807) never lost his sense of amazement at what Christ had done for him. In one of his hymns, he speaks about the amazing grace that had saved a wretch like himself. Nevertheless, the idea in this alleged saying hardly seems attributable to Jesus, since he came into the world not to be its judge but to be its saviour (John 3.17). True, he was amazed at the unbelief of the people (Mark 6.6) and at the hardness of their hearts, but not at the love of God which he came to proclaim and to enact. The purpose of his coming into the world was to seek and to save the lost (Luke 19.10).

17.28 – Abu Sa'id al-Kharkushi 257b
[Asin 162]   c

**The world is related to the future life
like a man who has two wives:
if he pleases one he will displease the other.**

Such a saying could have been spoken only in a society where
polygamy was allowed. It was not definitely forbidden among
Jews until about AD 1000 and still persists among them in
Islamic countries. The difficulty of pleasing two wives is similar
to the impossibility of a slave serving two masters (Matthew
6.24; Luke 16.13; *Thomas* 47 – 12.22).

17.29 – al-Ghazzali, Right Way of Devotions 63.14
(*eleventh / twelfth centuries*)
[Asin 176]   D

**How many lamps has the wind extinguished!
How many servants of God has vanity corrupted!**

Only those who endure to the end will be saved (Mark 13.13).
Yet, as John Bunyan observed, there is a way to hell from the
very gate of heaven. In two other Arabic sayings already
examined (17.16, 25), there is a picture of a lamp placed on the
flat roof of a house. Presumably, such a lamp could easily be
extinguished by the wind.

---

8 A Bridge from Time to Eternity

In 1849, an Arabic saying was discovered by the Scottish
missionary, Alexander Duff, over a vast gateway in the ruins of
Fatehpur Sikri (City of Victory), 110 miles south of Delhi.[12]

17.30 – The Arabic Bridge Saying   B

**Jesus, on whom be peace, has said:
The world is a bridge.**

Pass over it
but do not build your dwellings upon it.

This inscription was placed over the entrance to a huge mosque in 1601 by the Grand Mogul Abkar, Emperor of India, as a memorial of the day when he made triumphal entry into his former capital.

Abkar was well known for his interest in various religions. Recognizing the imperfections of each, he had placed in his private chapel images of Abraham and Christ, as well as of the legendary Greek poet, Orpheus, and the philosopher and mystic, Apollonius of Tyana (born about 4 BC). His wife was a Christian.

Abkar summoned to his court a Portuguese missionary to expound Christianity to him and tried to establish a religion made up of paganism, Islam and Christianity.

This was Abkar's dream, immortalized in verse by Alfred Lord Tennyson. In the course of a long poem entitled, 'Abkar's Dream', which was inspired by this inscription found by Alexander Duff, Abkar is made to say:

> There is light in all,
> And light, with more or less of shade, in all
> Man-modes of worship.

Alexander Duff recorded later the peculiar emotions with which he gazed at the curious inscription and then at the ruined buildings which had once been Abkar's palaces replenished with all the grandeur and glory of the greatest and wisest of Asiatic sovereigns. 'Poor Abkar! he built his dwellings on the bridge!'

This bridge saying occurs twice in al-Ghazzali's *Revival of the Religious Sciences* (**17.6**), once on its own and once as part of a longer discussion between Jesus and his disciples.

Traces of it have been found in a book by a Spanish Jew, Moses Sephardi, personal physician to King Alphonso I of Aragon (1105–34). At his baptism, he took the name of Petrus Alphonsi. One of the books he wrote was a collection of stories and proverbs to be used as sermon illustrations. At the end, there are Oriental sayings attributed to a philosopher about the end of life, including: 'The world is like a bridge. Pass over it, but do not settle on it.'

The saying can be traced even further back to one of the companions of Mohammed, Ibn 'Omar, who gives it as having come down through Mohammed from Jesus. It is thus one of the oldest of the Arabic sayings of Jesus.

Jeremias[13] doubted its authenticity on the ground that it contains no reference to the coming kingdom of God. Others have accepted it as being probably the most genuine of all the Arabic sayings attributed to Jesus. According to tradition, Thomas preached in India and founded the church in Travancore. The saying may have been a fragment of his teaching that was handed down by word of mouth in that area.

It has been pointed out that there were no bridges in Palestine and that the word for bridge does not occur in the Bible. Nevertheless, the saying could be genuine. It is possible that it dates from the visit of Jesus and his disciples to Phoenicia, when he cured a Syrophoenician woman's daughter (Mark 7.24–30). They would have been within sight of the famous mole or bridge which joined Tyre to the mainland. It was built by Alexander the Great in 332 BC in order to allow his army to attack the island fortress of Tyre and deprive the Persian fleet of its most important naval base on the Mediterranean coast. This spectacular causeway was over half-a-mile long and 200 feet broad.[14]

The warning in this saying is very like the teaching of Jesus in, for example, the parable of the rich fool (Luke 12.16–21; *Thomas* 63 – 9.7). One can also compare the shortest saying in Thomas: 'Become passers-by' (12.20). The world is like a stage leading to greater things. As Alexander the Great's army passed over the causeway and destroyed the fortress of Tyre as the prelude to conquering the whole of the known world of that time, so Christians are encouraged by Jesus to remember the transitoriness of this world as they pass through it on their way from time to eternity.

Part Five

What Have We Discovered?

CHAPTER EIGHTEEN

Gathering Up the Fragments

1 Pearls of Wisdom

It is only natural that people should be interested in the stray and half-forgotten pearls of wisdom that have fallen from the lips of a truly great man. How much truer must that be of Jesus.[1] Even the temple police sent to arrest him had to confess: 'No human being ever spoke thus' (John 7.46). As the disciples were told after the feeding of the Galilean crowd, I have attempted to gather up the remaining fragments (John 6.12) and to separate the gold from the dross. Of 383 sayings examined in the course of research, many have been omitted from this book, including the majority of the Arabic sayings, as being of very doubtful authenticity.[2] We have been left with 253 fragments (Table 3), of which 26 occur more than once (see doublets – Tables 3 and 5). When one also takes account of the fact that 76 of these are already known to us from the New Testament (Table 4), 151 sayings remain, but only 11 of these can be graded A and 25 have been graded B. The vast majority (115) are either insufficiently attested to be assigned with confidence to Jesus (C) or are of doubtful authenticity (D).

2 Why so few Gems?

Apart from the sayings in the Coptic *Gospel of Thomas*, many of which have parallels or echoes within the four canonical gospels, it is surprising how little of value survives outside the New Testament. The ministry of Jesus lasted approximately three years. Yet the canonical gospels, which give the impression of

201

Book Part	Grade				Totals
	A	B	C	D	
Table 3 **Spread and Grading of Sayings**					
II	12	5	14	7	38
III	53	15	29	21	118[3]
IV.13–16	13	17	18	19	67
IV.17	0	3	17	10	30
Totals	78	40	78	57	253
Less Doublets	9	3	8	6	26
Net Totals	69	37	70	51	227
New Testament (Table 4)	58	12	6	0	76
Otherwise Unknown (Table 5)	11	25	64	51	151

almost continuous teaching with short intervals of rest, are relatively short. How is it that several volumes of sayings are not available? Did not John declare that, if everything were written down, the whole world could not contain the books that would be written (John 21.25)?

The scarcity of material is even more surprising when we recall that it was an age of oral tradition. Memories were better than they are today. Those who heard the extraordinary words of

Book Part	Grade				Totals
	A	B	C	D	
Table 4 **New Testament Parallels**					
II	9	2	2	0	13
III	44	7	3	0	54[4]
IV.13–16	5	2	1	0	8
IV.17	0	1	0	0	1
Totals	58	12	6	0	76

Book Part	Grade				Totals
	A	B	C	D	
II	3	3	12	7	25
III	9	8	26	21	64
IV.13–16	8	15	17	19	59
IV.17	0	2	17	10	29
Totals	20	28	72	57	177
Less Doublets	9	3	8	6	26
Net Totals	11	25	64	51	151

Table 5
Otherwise Unknown Sayings

Jesus would surely have repeated them over and over again to friends and neighbours. Would someone not have thought of committing them to writing before the death of those who actually heard them for the first time? After all, this is the reason why the four gospels themselves came to be composed.

Part of the explanation may be the manner in which Jesus entrusted his teaching to twelve apostles. They – and they alone – were to be responsible for the spread of the gospel in the first instance. Anything that could not be traced back through them was quickly forgotten and lost in the mists of time. Much even of the so-called apocryphal material has survived because of association with the name of one of the original apostles.

3 Pure Gold

When we apply the tests of authenticity to the sayings that we have collected in this book, not a great deal of gold remains sifted from the dross[5] – but enough to have made the effort worthwhile. Of the 253 sayings examined, 78 have been graded A, 40 B, 78 C and 57 D as being of doubtful authenticity. When one takes account of the fact that many occur more than once, only about 69 sayings remain within grade A and 37 in grade B. Of these 106 graded A or B, the majority are already familiar to us from the New Testament. Only a very few genuine *agrapha* remain in the sense of sayings not written within the canonical books. How does this result compare with other collections made in the past hundred years?

4 Digging for Gold

From 1893 onwards, Alfred Resch made an exhaustive search of all the available sources, apart from Arabic, and published a total of 291 sayings. This included several from the Oxyrhynchus Papyri (6.2, 3, 5, 6, 8–11, 13, 14) but none from the Coptic *Gospel of Thomas* since it had not yet been discovered. Resch considered that 75 of the 291 sayings he had collected were probably genuine. His opinion was not generally accepted (see Table 7).[6]

Table 6
Views on Authenticity
A: Codes for Authors

Code	Author	Book or Article	Ref.	Date
1	J. H. Ropes	Fourteen Genuine Sayings	**18.5**	1896
2	B. Jackson	Twenty-five Agrapha	**18.6**	1900
3	J. H. Ropes	Ten Valuable Sayings	**17.4**	1904
4	David Smith	Unwritten Sayings	**18.8**	1913
5	J. Jeremias	Unknown Sayings	**18.9**	1957
6	A. M. Hunter	Unfamiliar Sayings	**18.10**	1963
7	O. Hofius	Revision of Jeremias	**18.11**	1982

5 Fourteen Genuine Sayings

James Hardy Ropes of Harvard University Divinity School undertook a critical consideration of the material gathered together by Alfred Resch.[7] In his 1896 study in German of the sayings of Jesus which are not handed down in the canonical gospels, he pruned Resch's list to 154. Of these, he concluded that 14 were likely to have been genuine sayings – 4.2; 4.4; 4.5; 4.10; 15.4; 15.5; 15.13; 16.4; 16.9, 28; 16.11, 19; 16.12, 18, 23; Revelation 16.15; grieving brother; Micah 1.7 (see **18.7**).

6 Twenty-five Agrapha

In a book published by SPCK in 1900, Blomfield Jackson collected what he considered to be the best authenticated extra-canonical sayings of Jesus.[8] He discussed in detail 25 such sayings and included some other supposed sayings – 14 in all – in an appendix. In his preface, he wrote that the treatment of the subject in the works of Resch and Ropes was exhaustive, but that their contents were not available to the English reader.

7 Ten Valuable Sayings

In Hastings' *Dictionary of the Bible* (1904),[9] J. H. Ropes collected 66 sayings from various sources and added on from Arabic writers another 48 of those listed by Margoliouth (**17.4**) and another three quoted by Levinus Warnerus, a seventeenth-century Christian writer (17.15), giving a total of 117. Of the first 66, Ropes regarded only 10 as seeming with considerable probability to possess historical value, not 14 as he had previously done (**18.5**) – 4.2; 4.4; 4.5; 4.10; 15.13; 16.9, 28; 16.11, 19; 16.12, 18, 23; grieving brother; Micah 1.7. The second last is quoted from the *Gospel of the Nazaraeans* (**15.2**) but is not actually said to be from Jesus, and the last is a quotation from Micah 1.7 put into his mouth in the *Mishnah*, a Jewish document dating from the second century A D. Ropes declared that the *agrapha* (unwritten sayings) from Islamic sources were chiefly of merely curious interest.

8 Unwritten Sayings

In a series of lectures at McCrea Magee College in Londonderry about 1913, David Smith considered in detail eight unwritten sayings of Jesus (4.7; 16.9; 16.13; 17.30; 6.5; 16.12; 16.14; 6.20) and referred briefly to another three (4.2; 4.10; 12.33). While admitting that these sayings 'lack the sanction of the holy evangelists and of none of them is it possible to be assured that it is his very word', nevertheless David Smith was certain that the truths they express were those of Jesus and that 'if he spoke through these words to the hearts of believers long ago, he will speak likewise to ours'.[10]

9 Unknown Sayings

In 1957, Joachim Jeremias wrote that, while there were many unwritten sayings in the *Gospel of Thomas*, that work yielded

Ref	Saying	Those accepting authenticity							My Grade
		Table 7 **Views on Authenticity** B: Sayings							
4.2	Giving	1	2	3	4		6		B
4.4	Lord's coming	1		3		5			C
4.5	Little/less	1	2	3					B
4.7	Sabbath		2		4	5	6	7	A
4.10	Adulteress	1		3	4		6		B
6.2	Fasting/sabbath		2						C
6.3	Stood in midst		2						D
6.5	Wood/stone		2		4	(5)	6		A
6.6	Prophet/doctor						6		A
6.16	Clothing					5	6		B
6.17	On guard					5			C
6.20	Temple				4	5	6	7	C
6.21	Enemies					5		7	A
9.1	Fisherman					5		7	A
12.20	Passers-by					5			A
12.33 16.20	Near Fire		2		4	5	6	7	A
14.4	Not understood				5				B
15.1	Sinless Jesus		2						C
15.3	Forgiving					5			B
15.4	Rich Man	1				5			B
15.5	Worthy	1	2						C
15.9	No Sacrifices		2						D
15.10	Holy Spirit/Mother		2						D
15.11	Wonder/reigns		2						C
15.13	Love/joy	1	2	3		5	6	7	B
15.14	Bring table		2						C
16.4	Wolves/lambs	1							B
16.7	Two/one		2						D

16.8	Divisions		2			5			A
16.9 16.26	Judging	1	2	3	4	5	6	7	A
16.10	Vines springing up		2						C
16.11 16.18	Big things	1	2	3		5	6	7	A
16.12 16.22	Money-changers	1	2	3	4	5	6	7	A
16.13	Wonder/Knowledge				4				B
16.14	My mystery		2		4				C
16.15	Temptation					5	6		B
16.16	Save self					5			C
16.17	Weak, hungry		2						C
16.19	Sodom justified		2						C
16.21	Weak saved through strong		2						C
16.34	Proclaim my Death		2						B
17.13	Dead Dog's Teeth						6		C
17.30	Bridge				4	(5)	6		B

very little for his purpose of collecting the unknown sayings of Jesus. In the end, he was left with a residue from all sources of only 21 sayings whose attestation and subject-matter did not give rise to objections of weight. These 21 were perfectly compatible with the synoptic tradition, he maintained, and their authenticity admitted of serious consideration.[11]

After careful examination, Jeremias eventually rejected 2 of these 21 sayings since their historical authenticity was improbable or out of the question. He regarded them as being the creations of Christian prophecy. These were the saying about the stone and the wood (6.5; 11.17) and the bridge saying (17.30).[12] He quoted J. H. Ropes as saying that 'only here and there, amid a mass of worthless rubbish, do we come across a priceless jewel.' While admitting that Ropes probably went too far and that the value of the extra-canonical tradition must be placed a little higher than it was by Ropes, nevertheless for Jeremias the real value of these sayings outside the four gospels lay in the fact that they throw into sharp relief the unique value of the canonical gospels themselves. 'The lost dominical sayings may supplement our knowledge here and there in important and valuable ways, but they cannot do more than that.'[13]

10 Unfamiliar Sayings

In an essay on the unfamiliar sayings of Jesus, published in 1963, A. M. Hunter summed up the position by saying that 'a succession of scholars from Alfred Resch to Joachim Jeremias have gathered and sifted these sayings with minute and scholarly care. The result is to leave us with twelve to twenty sayings which seem to pass all tests with flying colours and may be regarded as genuine.'[14] From this total, Professor Hunter picked out some 'vivid and valuable' examples for exposition – 4.2; 4.7; 4.10; 6.5; 6.16; 6.20; 12.33 (16.20); 15.13; 16.9, 28; 16.15; 6.21; 16.12; 6.16; 16.11. He also referred briefly to 6.6 (11.6); 17.13 and 17.30.

11 Revision of Jeremias

More recently (1982), the evidence for the 18 sayings accepted by Joachim Jeremias has been reassessed by Otfried Hofius.[15] He concluded that only 9 of them had strong claims to authenticity – 6.20; 16.9, 28; 9.1; 16.11, 19; 16.12, 18, 23; 4.7; 12.33, 16.20; 15.13; 6.21.

12 Extra-canonical Sayings

In 1989, William Stroker was less concerned about the search for authentic sayings than with collecting all the available material in their original languages as a contribution to the study of the stages that led to the formation of the canonical gospels.[16] He classified sayings as apophthegms (pithy sayings), parables, prophetic and apocalyptic sayings, wisdom sayings, I-sayings (in which Jesus speaks using the first person singular) and community rules. While he considered his collection to be the most extensive so far published, he deliberately omitted sayings in Islamic literature as being so numerous as to be virtually a book in themselves.

13 Are these the Words of Jesus?

In a book with this catching title, published in 1990, Ian Wilson has presented what he regards as dramatic evidence from beyond the New Testament. He assesses the respective claims to authenticity of many of the sayings we have considered in this present collection. While he does not consider all the material in the Coptic *Gospel of Thomas*, he believes that it does contain several credible-sounding sayings unknown from any other source. The version of some Thomas sayings with synoptic parallels 'often seems to provide a simpler, and therefore arguably more original form'.[17] Yet he concludes that it has undergone serious tampering at gnostic hands.

14 Gathering up Fragments from Thomas

By reclaiming the Coptic *Gospel of Thomas* from gnosticism and placing it in the context of Syriac Christianity, it has been possible to gain from it something of value for the interpretation of canonical sayings of Jesus, especially the parables. In certain cases, this collection may preserve in a form independent of the New Testament, material that is more primitive and closer to the original words of Jesus. As James Robinson predicted in 1959, 'an increase in the quantity of authentic sayings of Jesus may be reasonably expected'.[18]

15 Fresh Light on Canonical Sayings

In chapters 6 and 9 to 12, we have discovered several sayings from the Greek and Coptic versions of the *Gospel of Thomas* that may contain primitive material.

This is a possibility, for example, with regard to the doctor not healing those who know him in *Thomas* 31 (11.6) and Oxyrhynchus Papyrus 1 (6.6).

The shorter form of the saying about the speck and the log in *Thomas* 26 (12.13) could be more primitive than that in Matthew 7.3–5 and Luke 6.41f.

In *Thomas* 32 (12.14) the poetic parallelism of the saying about a city on a high mountain being fortified points in the same direction.

Thomas 54 (9.20) may preserve the original form of the beatitude on the poor.

By detaching the metaphor about the rejected corner-stone in *Thomas* 66 (11.7) from the parable of the tenants in *Thomas* 65 (9.9), *Thomas* may be pointing to the fact that originally it was a floating saying and not part and parcel of the parable as it was told by Jesus.

Can dogs throw what is holy on the dungheap? Perhaps the reference in *Thomas* 93 (12.28) is rather to people who are unable to receive the message of the gospel. In any case, the extra words indicate that the compiler of *Thomas* was writing independently of Matthew's Gospel.

The three-fold statement about the things of Caesar, of God and of Jesus in *Thomas* 100 (12.29) could be authentic, even though it is not made clear what comprises the last category.

16 Fresh Light on Canonical Parables

In particular, as far as the Coptic *Gospel of Thomas* is concerned, the independent versions of twelve New Testament parables may, in several cases, throw fresh light on the text and the teaching of these familiar stories. Whatever brings us closer to the mind and the message of Jesus is to be welcomed.

In the parable of the wise fisherman in *Thomas* 8 (9.1), there is a casting-net rather than a dragnet as in Matthew 13.47. Moreover, the point of the parable as the joy of a great discovery rather than the mixture of people in the kingdom of heaven could be original.

The variant reading in *Thomas* 9 (9.2) makes more sense of the agricultural process with seed falling upon the trodden path instead of neatly beside the road.

The unpairing of the parables of the mustard seed in *Thomas* 20 (9.3) and of the leaven in *Thomas* 96 (9.11) may point to the fact that they were originally told on different occasions and that their appearance together in Matthew 13 was due to the editorial work of the evangelist.

In the parable of the leaven in *Thomas* 96 (9.11), Jesus compares the kingdom of heaven to what happens when a woman takes leaven and hides it in dough. Jesus often compared God's reign to what people do in certain circumstances – a farmer sowing seed, a woman sweeping out her house in her search for a lost coin, a father waiting for his prodigal son to return home, a shepherd going out after a lost sheep. Moreover, the contrast between the little beginning and the large ending is brought out better in the version in *Thomas* than in its canonical parallel, with the presence of the adjectives little and large – a little leaven producing large loaves (9.11).

In the parable of the tenants in *Thomas* 65 (9.9), the series of three messengers sent by the owner of the vineyard may be more original. The story comes to a climax with murder amongst the vines since only the owner's son was killed by the tenants.

The description of a general merchant who found a pearl by accident in *Thomas* 76 (9.10) presents a more likely picture than that of a pearl merchant who sold all that he had on finding one pearl of great value (Matthew 13.45f.).

The story of a shepherd going out after a lost sheep in *Thomas* 107 (9.14) has theological insights not found in the canonical parallels in Matthew and in Luke. God's unceasing efforts for the salvation of Jews as well as Gentiles is portrayed in memorable language.

While the parable of the hidden treasure in *Thomas* 109 (9.15) may present us with a more complicated version (so graded C), it has an unexpected twist at the end with the final owner showing his joy and his confidence by lending money to whomever he wished.

17 New Parables

Such fresh light on the teaching of Jesus is not confined to these stories already known to us from the New Testament. Even although it is impossible to argue for the authenticity of the three new parables wholeheartedly and grade them as A, they may contain hidden treasure also. The parable of the woman with the jar of meal in *Thomas* 97 (9.12) is not to be immediately dismissed. Nor should the parable of the assassin

(9.13) be rejected without hesitation. The parable of the little children taking off their clothes in a field (9.4) may seem the most unlikely of the three.

18 A Handful of Silver

From the Jewish-Christian gospels comes a handful of silver. Two sayings that may well be authentic show Jesus desirous of accepting baptism from John (15.7) and acknowledging those who do the Father's will as being his true relatives (15.8), both echoing Matthew's Gospel.

Also significant are alternative renderings of daily bread in the Lord's Prayer as tomorrow's bread or bread essential to existence (15.2) and the linking of Christian joy with brotherly love (15.13). The picture of a second rich man scratching his head over the command of Jesus to sell all and give to the poor lends a vivid touch to the incident while Jesus' further elucidation makes it clear that it is the selfish use of riches that is being condemned, not their possession (15.4).

We can be grateful to early Christian writers like Clement of Alexandria and Origen for bringing to our attention such sayings as those about money-changers (16.12, 22), about asking for the big things (16.11, 18) and about the inevitability of suffering in the Christian life (16.20; 12.33); and for reminding us of the importance of a sense of wonder as the gateway to knowledge (16.13).

19 Arabic Gems

Arabic gems are few and far between; but they are there for the finding.

First of all, there are at least two in the Koran. The command of Jesus to fear God and to obey himself (17.3) could be taken as a motto by Christians as also the promise of the disciples to be God's helpers (17.1, 5).

From al-Ghazzali's collection come an extension to the maxim about pearls and pigs (17.8), the comment of Jesus about the white teeth of a dead dog (17.13), the impossibility of mixing fire and water (17.14), the danger of drinking sea water (17.15), and the interesting expansion of the saying about anxiety to include camels (17.19).

The comparisons of a blind man carrying a lamp (17.25) and of a lamp placed on the roof of a dark house (17.16) with speaking wisely but acting foolishly, the reference to amazing grace (17.27), the impossibility of a man pleasing two wives (17.28), lamps being extinguished by the wind (17.29), the picturesque condemnation of gossiping (17.10) – all these and other gems, whether deemed authentic or not, can be culled from various Moslem writers. Whether rightly or wrongly attributed to Jesus, they provide colourful pictures of eternal truth. Above all, the Arabic bridge saying attested by a variety of sources (17.30) provides a fitting conclusion to our survey of hidden treasure.

20 Be careful how you hear

While much fine gold may be rescued from the mass of sayings attributed to Jesus, some scholars have drawn misleading conclusions. They have seen presented here a radically different view of Christianity, especially in the Coptic works discovered at Chenoboskion. In particular, the Coptic *Gospel of Thomas* has been tarred with the same brush as the rest of the Nag Hammadi Library and has been regarded as a thoroughly gnostic document. This has led to a distorted view of early Christianity.

21 A Gospel without Good News

Elaine Pagels has argued (1979) that gnostic Christianity taught a true equality of all, both male and female.[19] Immediate religious experience was available to everyone without the necessity of having professional clergy. The resurrection of Jesus was unimportant, since enlightenment or knowledge alone could bring awareness of his spiritual presence. There is no need for a doctrine of atonement – the way in which Jesus brought God and humankind together by means of his death on the cross. There is no such thing as sin, only darkness. This can be obliterated by means of self-knowledge. There is no need for the

213

forgiveness of sins by God. What Professor Pagels has presented is a gospel without any good news.

22 A Gnostic Sermon

More recently (1992), another attempt to find in the Coptic *Gospel of Thomas* a watered-down Christianity has been made in the interpretation offered by Harold Bloom.[20] According to this reading of the text, Thomas spares us the crucifixion, makes the resurrection unnecessary and does not present us with a God named Jesus. Instead, we have a dogma-free religion that has nothing to do with the institutional Church or with the creeds of orthodox Christianity. While Marvin Meyer refuses to label the sayings in *Thomas* as gnostic, Harold Bloom has no hesitation in calling his commentary a gnostic sermon. Using this new trans-lation as his text, he regards ignorance as the main human problem and its replacement by self-knowledge as the remedy.

23 Be Skilled Money-changers

All such travesties must be firmly rejected. We must take to heart the oft-repeated conclusion to sayings of Jesus both in the New Testament and in *Thomas*, 'Let whoever has ears to hear, hear!' (9.1). In the words of the saying preserved by many early writers including Clement of Alexandria (16.12), Origen (**16.9**) and the *Clementine Homilies* (16.22), we have to be skilled money-changers, rightly sifting the gold and the silver from the counterfeit. Only so can we be sure that what we have found is really hidden treasure.

24 The Portrait of Jesus

In our discussion of methods of studying the New Testament, we saw that some scholars have doubted the possibility of knowing anything at all about Jesus (**3.5**). In spite of such hesitations, it can be maintained that the canonical gospels do give us a reliable picture of his life and teaching. We are now ready to ask a further question, What kind of Jesus are we left with after our study of sayings outside the four gospels? Has he been shown in a radically new light?

214

If one leaves aside ascetic and encratitic sayings from *Thomas* that seem to have originated in, or been influenced by, the Christian community at Edessa in Syria (e.g., 9.17; 9.19; 10.26; 10.27; 12.6; 12.8; 15.17; 16.30) and also fanciful tales that are clearly sensational (e.g., 13.1; 13.2; 15.10), the picture that emerges is broadly in line with the portraits drawn by New Testament writers, provided one does not attempt to read gnosticism into documents where it is not already clearly present (e.g., 9.1; 9.3; 9.26; 10.2; 10.29; 11.8; 12.15; 12.29; 14.1).

In Q, the sayings source lying behind Matthew and Luke (**3.2**), Jesus was regarded as a wise man or as a child of Wisdom, as we see from Luke 7.35 – 'Wisdom has been justified by all her children', including Jesus and John the Baptist. For Matthew, on the other hand, the deeds of Jesus the Messiah (Matthew 11.2) were the deeds of Wisdom (Matthew 11.19). Moreover, Matthew puts into the mouth of Jesus a similar invitation to that found in the mouth of Wisdom, an abridged form of which appears in *Thomas* 90 (11.14). In other words, Jesus is not simply a wise man (12.2) who enunciates pearls of wisdom in the form of parables, pithy sayings and long discourses. He is the wisdom of God in human form, according to Matthew and *Thomas* as well as Paul (**2.4**; 1 Corinthians 1.24, 30; 10.3; 11.9; 11.14).[21]

Jesus is also the living one (10.30; 10.41; 11.13), who existed before his birth (9.18; 14.10) and who continues to be with his disciples in their daily life and work in the world (6.5; 11.16; 11.17; 13.2). He is the light that is above them all (11.17). His sinlessness is taken for granted (5.1; 10.23; 15.1; 15.7).

He is the Son of man (11.8; 14.9; 15.14) and the Son of the living one (12.7), who is equal with the Father (10.35; 11.4) and the divine authority of whose teaching is implied (11.1), even in Arabic sayings taken from Moslem sources (**17.2**).

Of course, as far as Mohammed was concerned, there is no question of his equality with God. He is simply one of the prophets (**17.2**). In the Koran, Jesus is referred to as son of Mary (**17.3**; 17.5).

25 The Teaching of Jesus

The main advantage gained from our study has been the fresh

light shed on the teaching of Jesus, especially with regard to parables (18.16; 18.17). In addition, a few colourful and vivid sayings have been discovered that are otherwise unknown to us (18.18; 18.19).

The transitoriness of human life on earth (9.4; 12.20; 17.20) and the folly of setting one's heart on material possessions (9.7; 10.6; 10.7; 10.8; 12.20; 14.11; 15.4; 16.27; 16.30; 17.14; 17.15) have been two of the main lessons stressed over and over again, not least in the Arabic bridge saying (17.30).

26 The Challenge of Jesus

Further analysis of the sayings could be dangerous. One of the main criteria of authenticity that has been applied is compatability with what we already know of Jesus from the canonical gospels (3.11; 3.13). Nevertheless, even those that have been rejected as unlikely to be genuine (C and D) have, in at least certain cases, shown similarities to the general outline obtained from biblical documents.

In the end, the individual is left to make up his or her own mind as to who Jesus is. 'Tell me whom I am like.' (*Thomas* 13 – 12.2) 'Who do you say that I am?' (Matthew 16.15) 'Happy are you, who believed in me without having seen me' (Letter to Abgar the Great – 13.3). 'Let whoever has ears to hear, hear' (9.1; 9.9; etc.). Or, as this has been rendered in the Scholars Version: 'Anyone with two good ears had better listen!'[22]

Notes

Full details of books referred to here by short titles can be found in the Suggestions for Further Reading.

Chapter One

1. Wand, *History*, pp. 50–2.
2. Hunter, *Introducing*, pp. 22–5.
3. In an article in *Expository Times* 86 (1974/5), pp. 132–6, as one in a series on 'New Wine in Old Wineskins', I discuss the idea of the covenant as one of the golden threads running through the great tapestry of the Bible.

Chapter Two

1. This is the perfect participle passive of the verb *kruptein* = 'to hide'; so it means literally, 'having been hidden'.
2. Davies, *Thomas*, pp. 2f.: 'There is a general consensus among scholars that of all the non-canonical Christian writings we possess, the Gospel of Thomas contains the most authentic record of the teachings of Jesus.'
3. Crossan, *Four Other Gospels*, p. 10; compare Tuckett, *Reading*, p. 10, who declares that, when we study primitive Christianity and its literature as a part of ancient history, 'many of us will ignore the limits of the Christian canon completely. We may decide that information about Jesus can be found in the *Gospel of Thomas* as well as in the *Gospel of Mark*; the fact that Mark is in the canon and Thomas is not will not make a scrap of difference to those who are trying to recover reliable information about Jesus.'

Chapter Three

1. Streeter, *Four Gospels*. A. M. Hunter regarded this book as the finest on this subject in any language (*Interpreting*, p. 40); while John Kloppenborg (*Formation of Q*, p. 17) describes it as 'the classic British formulation of the two-document hypothesis'. For a clear summary of this solution to the literary puzzle, see Hunter, *Introducing*, pp. 34–9.
2. Recent studies on Q include David Catchpole, *The Quest for Q* (T. & T. Clark 1993); Piper, *Gospel behind Gospels*; C. M. Tuckett, *Studies on Q* (T. & T. Clark 1995).

3. An earlier solution proposed by Johann Griesbach (1745–1812) that Mark was the last gospel to be written, making use of Matthew and Luke as sources, has been revived by some scholars in modern times. In addition, the four-document theory was challenged by M. D. Goulder in *Midrash and Lection in Matthew* (SPCK 1974). He maintains that Matthew is a midrashic expansion of Mark and so does away with the necessity of postulating the existence of hypothetical documents such as Q and M. Similarly, Luke used Matthew in the composition of his gospel (M. D. Goulder, *Luke: a New Paradigm*, Sheffield Academic Press 1989). For a detailed examination of Goulder's views and a strong defence of the existence of Q, see C. M. Tuckett, 'The Existence of Q', in Piper, *Gospel behind Gospels*, pp. 19–47. For a more complicated solution to the synoptic problem which suggests the existence of various editions of the sources, see Sanders and Davies, *Synoptic Gospels*.

4. Stanton, *Gospel Truth?* p. 55.

5. R. Bultmann, *Jesus and the Word* (Nicholson & Watson 1935), p. 9: 'We can, strictly speaking, know nothing of the person of Jesus.' Compare R. H. Lightfoot, *History and Interpretation in the Gospels* (Hodder & Stoughton 1935), p. 225: 'The form of the earthly no less than of the heavenly Christ is for the most part hidden from us. For all the inestimable value of the gospels, they yield us little more than a whisper of his voice; we trace in them but the outskirts of his ways.'

6. According to a group of scholars meeting as the Jesus Seminar, 'Eighty-two percent of the words ascribed to Jesus in the gospels were not actually spoken by him' (Funk, *Five Gospels*, p. 15). This may have been over-sceptical.

7. Black, *Aramaic Approach*; J. Jeremias, *New Testament Theology* vol. 1 *The Proclamation of Jesus*, Part One: *How Reliable is the Tradition of the Sayings of Jesus?* (SCM Press 1971); see further Loren T. Stuckenbruck, 'An Approach to the New Testament through Aramaic Sources: the Recent methodological Debate', in *Journal for the Study of the Pseudepigrapha* 8 (1991), pp. 3–29, who writes: 'Today it is widely assumed that if Jesus and his early followers spoke at least some Aramaic and Hebrew, then inevitably parts of the Greek text should reflect a process of translation and interpretation within the early Christian communities' (p. 3).

8. Kloppenborg, *Formation of Q*, pp. 51–64, argues strongly for Greek as the original language of Q with some Aramaic words. Stanton, *Gospel Truth?* p. 64, considers that, 'since there is often close verbal correspondence in Matthew's and Luke's Q traditions, it is probable that they were both drawing on traditions in the same language, i.e. Greek.'

9. C. H. Dodd, *Historical Tradition in the Fourth Gospel* (Cambridge

University Press 1963); Hunter, *John*, pp. 78–89; Hunter, *Parables*, p. 9.

10. See Robinson, *Priority*; Hunter, *John*, pp. 90–101. For a valuable survey of studies on John's Gospel, see Stephen Smalley's article in *Expository Times* 97 (1985/6), pp. 102–8.

11. W. L. Briscoe, *A Comparison of the Parables in the Gospel according to Thomas and the Synoptic Gospels* (PhD thesis: Southwestern Baptist Theological Seminary 1965), wrote of the parables in *Thomas*, that they represent 'not trustworthy, independent tradition of the synoptic parables. As such, Thomas' versions represent not what Jesus said but what some men wished he had.'

12. Funk, *Five Gospels*, p. 15.

13. Compare Tuckett, *Reading*, p. 104.

14. Compare Hedrick, *Parables*, p. 251: 'We must begin synoptic criticism with the assumption that Thomas in principle preserves a valuable independent witness to the early Jesus tradition.' Funk, *Five Gospels*, p. 15: 'A significant new independent source of data for the study of the historical Jesus is the Gospel of Thomas.' Funk, *Five Gospels*, p. 26: 'Double attestation in the early independent sources Thomas and Q constitutes strong documentary evidence.'

Chapter Four

1. See, for example, Finegan, *Manuscripts*; Moulton, *Papyrus*; Stanton, *Gospel Truth?* pp. 33–48. The controversial view that three scraps of papyrus containing parts of some words from Matthew 26 (p^{64}) and usually dated to about AD 200 actually date from the middle of the first century has been ably refuted by Graham Stanton (*Gospel Truth?* pp. 1–19).

2. Compare Jackson, *Agrapha*, p. 13: 'The full force of the tense might be brought out by rendering, "It is blessed to be a giver rather than a receiver." '

3. Ropes, *Agrapha* (see chapter 18, note 8); E. Haenchen, *The Acts of the Apostles* (Blackwell 1972), p. 595. Jeremias declares that 'there can be no doubt that this is a real agraphon' (*Unknown Sayings*, p. 13) and then writes on pp. 32f.: 'The agraphon quoted in Acts 20.35 is probably a proverb current in the Graeco-Roman world and put into the mouth of Jesus.'

4. This is the view of Jeremias in *Eucharistic Words*, pp. 159–65.

5. Jeremias, *Unknown Sayings*, pp. 80–3.

6. See Ernest Best, *The First and Second Epistles to the Thessalonians* (A. & C. Black 1972), pp. 189–201; F. F. Bruce, *1 and 2 Thessalonians* (Word Books 1982), pp. 98–103. On the whole subject of the second coming, see T. F. Glasson, *Jesus and the End of the World* (Saint Andrew Press 1980).

7. Compare Moulton, *Papyrus*, p. 22: 'That sounds like a very genuine

saying of Christ, even though it is recorded nowhere else.' For a detailed discussion regarding its authenticity, see Jeremias, *Unknown Sayings*, pp. 61–5, who argues that much can be said in favour of the view that we have here an early tradition and that the mind of Jesus is betrayed in its combination of freedom and reverence, in the succinctness and gravity of the saying.

8. Streeter, *Four Gospels*, p. 277; Taylor, *Text*, pp. 24f.
9. Hunter, *Teaching and Preaching*, p. 27, drawing on an insight from T. W. Manson. Professor Hunter concluded: 'The Dominical dialectic in the cause of compassion was surely never more wonderfully displayed.'

Chapter Five

1. See H. I. Bell, *Recent Discoveries of Biblical Manuscripts* (Clarendon Press 1937); H. I. Bell and T. C. Skeat, *Fragments of an Unknown Gospel and other early Christian Papyri* (Oxford University Press 1935); Dodd, *Studies*, pp. 12–52; Crossan, *Four Other Gospels*, pp. 64–75.
2. See Crossan, *Four Other Gospels*, pp. 77–87.
3. Dodd, *Studies*, p. 43.

Chapter Six

1. See B. P. Grenfell and A. S. Hunt, *Oxyrhynchus Papyri* (Egyptian Exploration Fund 1898 and 1908); Hennecke vol. 1, pp. 97–116; Moulton, *Rubbish Heaps*; Milligan, *Here and There*.
2. Compare Hunter, *Teaching and Preaching*, p. 28; Jeremias, *Unknown Sayings*, pp. 47–60, who calls this story 'a pearl of gospel artistry'.

Chapter Seven

1. See sketch map.
2. Robinson, *Nag Hammadi*.
3. See *Pachomian Koinonia: the Lives, Rules and other Writings of Saint Pachomius and his Disciples*. Two volumes translated with an introduction by Armand Veilleux, Monk of Mistassini (Kalamazoo, Michigan: Cistercian Publications Inc. 1980).
4. But see J. C. O'Neill, 'The Origins of Monasticism' in R. D. Williams (ed.), *The Making of Orthodoxy* (Oxford University Press 1989), pp. 270–87, for the view that monasticism was always there in the Christian Church from the very beginning and that it was a continuation of Jewish monasticism. Compare A. Vööbus, *Celibacy, a Requirement for Admission to Baptism in the Early Syrian Church* (Stockholm 1951); *History of Asceticism in the Syrian Orient* (*Corpus Scriptorum Christianorum Orientalium* 184.14 1958), who argues that Syrian monasticism antedates the origin of monasticism in Egypt.

See Robinson and Koester, *Trajectories*, p. 125 note 21 and p. 126 note 23.

5. J. Doresse, *The Secret Books of the Egyptian Gnostics – an Introduction to the Gnostic Coptic Manuscripts discovered at Chenoboskion* (Hollis & Carter 1960), p. 83.
6. *Pachomian Koinonia* (note 3 above), vol. 2, p. 29.
7. See F. Wisse, 'Gnosticism and Early Monasticism in Egypt', in B. Aland (ed.), *Gnosis: Festschrift für Hans Jonas* (Vandenhoeck & Ruprecht 1978), pp. 431–40; T. Säve-Söderbergh, 'The Pagan Elements in Early Christianity and Gnosticism', in B. Barc (ed.), *Colloque international sur les textes de Nag Hammadi* (Quebec 1978, published 1981), pp. 71–85.
8. J. W. B. Barns, G. M. Browne and J. C. Shelton (eds.), *Nag Hammadi Codices: Greek and Coptic Papyri from the Cartonnage of the Covers* (Brill), pp. 15f., 105.
9. See *Pachomian Koinonia*, vol. 1, p. 368, where we read that, by this action of burning the dead monk's clothes, Pachomius put 'fear into all that they neglect not their life. How he put up with him till he died we do not know. But this we know, that men of God do nothing hurtful; and their severity as well as their goodness are measured by their knowledge of God.'

Chapter Eight
1. Guillaumont, *Thomas*; Layton, *Nag Hammadi*, pp. 38–93; Robinson, *Nag Hammadi*, pp. 117–30.
2. Koester (*Ancient Gospels*, p. 87) makes the synoptic parallels seventy-nine rather than sixty-six and declares that forty-six of these seventy-nine have Q parallels. Kloppenborg (*Q Thomas*, p. 159) lists forty Q-Thomas parallels.
3. Joachim Jeremias (*Parables*, p. 24) declared that the *Gospel of Thomas* provides us with an independent tradition for eleven of the synoptic parables, not twelve, since he regarded the parable of the fisherman (*Thomas* 8 – 9.1) as being without synoptic parallel.
4. This seems to be the way in which the sayings in Mark 9.34–50 have been put together, linked by the words 'child', 'name', 'fire', 'salt'. Compare Robinson and Koester, *Trajectories*, p. 136; A. K. Helmbold, *The Nag Hammadi Gnostic Texts and the Bible* (Baker Book House 1967), p. 57.
5. See Robinson and Koester, *Trajectories*, p. 136: 'Thomas does not use Q, but he does represent the eastern branch of the *Gattung, logoi*, the western branch being represented by the synoptic logoi of Q, which was used in western Syria by Matthew and later by Luke.'
6. Johannes von Leipoldt, 'Ein neues Evangelium? Das koptische Thomasevangelium übersetzt und besprochen', in *Theologische Literaturzeitung* vol. 83 (1958), column 496.

7. G. Quispel, 'Some Remarks on the Gospel of Thomas', in *New Testament Studies* 5 (1958/9), p. 277. Those who have supported the idea of the independence of *Thomas* include Vincent Taylor (*Text*, p. 14); and John Robinson (*Redating*, p. 451).
8. Patterson, *Thomas and Jesus*.
9. Stanton, *Gospel Truth?* pp. 84, 91.
10. See Crossan, *Four Other Gospels*, pp. 23–6, who believes that the *Gospel of Thomas* came from Edessa before AD 140 and that it was composed there as early as the middle of the first century AD; compare Koester and Robinson, *Trajectories*, pp. 127ff. See also Murray, *Symbols*, p. 4: 'A large number of scholars hold that Edessa was the cradle of Syriac Christianity.'
11. For a valuable survey of Tatian's *Diatessaron*, see William L. Peterson in Koester, *Ancient Gospels*, pp. 403–30.
12. Quispel (*Tatian and Thomas*, pp. 174–90) has drawn attention to over forty places in which *Thomas* and the *Diatessaron* agree in their readings. He accounted for this by suggesting that Tatian and *Thomas* both used the *Gospel according to the Hebrews* as a common source. William Peterson (Koester, *Ancient Gospels*, p. 428), while acknowledging that Tatian must have used a fifth source, prefers to assume the dependence of *Thomas* and Tatian on a common tradition.
13. This is the view of Koester in Robinson and Koester, *Trajectories*, p. 142.
14. J. H. Charlesworth, in the preface to his edition of the *Odes of Solomon* (Clarendon Press 1973), argues that this document is the earliest Christian hymn-book, dates it to around AD 100 and declares that it is older than any gnostic school of which we have clear knowledge.
15. In *Celibacy, a Requirement for Admission to Baptism in the Early Syrian Church* (Papers of the Estonian Theological Society in Exile) published in Stockholm in 1951, A. Vööbus draws attention to the Pseudo-Clementine *De Virginitate*, which gives a glimpse into the life and activity of Christians in Syria or Mesopotamia who, as baptized celibates, belonged to the membership of the Church.
16. For example, Grant, *Secret Sayings*. Stanton, *Jesus*, p. 131, concludes, 'From the whole thrust of Thomas, those addressed must be gnostics.' G. W. MacRae, 'Nag Hammadi and the New Testament', in B. Aland (ed.), *Gnosis: Festschrift für Hans Jonas* (Vandenhoeck & Ruprecht 1978), p. 152, says, 'I believe it is a thoroughly gnostic work though this has occasionally been challenged.' M. D. Goulder, *Luke: a new Paradigm* (Sheffield Academic Press 1989), vol. 1, p. 23 and vol. 2, p. 694, states, 'No serious attention should be given to Thomas, which is a gnosticizing version of the Gospels, especially Luke. . . . He (Thomas) is for ever abbreviating the Gospel material

for the sake of his gnostic mystifications.' Stanton, *Gospel Truth?* p. 87, holds that 'In its present form, Thomas is a gnostic writing, as are most of the writings of the Nag Hammadi Library.'

17. Those who have challenged the gnostic origin and character of *Thomas* include Quispel, *Tatian and Thomas*; and Davies, *Thomas*, p. 3., who says, 'If Thomas is gnostic, then perhaps Christians need pay little attention to it. But if it is not gnostic in any meaningful sense, then Christian scholarship has falsely denigrated and subsequently ignored a text of great importance. . . . In no meaningful sense is Thomas gnostic.' The most obvious gnostic themes and concepts are missing from *Thomas*. There are no references to aeons ('ages of the universe') and syzygies ('conjunctions' or 'oppositions'), or to the Demiurge, the gnostic name for the Creator of this universe, which being evil, could not have been created by a good God; or to the *Pleroma* ('the All'). But see *Thomas* 2, 67, 77, where the Coptic word for 'all things' is frequently mistranslated as 'the All', as if it were a gnostic technical term: see below, Chapter 10, note 4.

18. See Quispel, *Tatian and Thomas*, p. 103.

19. See E. A. Judge, 'The Earliest Use of *Monachos* for Monk and the Origins of Monasticism', in *Jahrbuch für Antike und Christentum* (Münster Westfalen), vol. 20 (1977), pp. 72–9.

Chapter Nine

1. This difference of method in classification may appear rather arbitrary. Parables and beatitudes could have been classified according to their themes and considered in one of the other chapters. However, it has seemed useful to isolate parables and beatitudes, since these are clearly identifiable forms. In addition, the parables are one of the most important contributions of *Thomas* to the whole area of New Testament study.

2. Helmut Koester (Robinson and Koester, *Trajectories*, p. 175) considers that 'perhaps all are original parables of Jesus' and that this is also not improbable for the parables which lack parallels in the synoptic gospels' (note 56). He goes on to say: 'I presuppose that the parables of Thomas are not taken from the synoptic gospels, but derive from an earlier stage of the tradition of synoptic parables' (p. 176).

3. In an article in *Expository Times* 95 (1983/4), pp. 269–73, 281f., I considered in detail the light shed on the canonical parable by this version in *Thomas*.

4. This suggestion, made by G. Quispel in 'Some Remarks on the Gospel of Thomas', in *New Testament Studies* 5 (1958/9), p. 289, seems more likely than that of Claus-Hunno Hunzinger in 'Unbekannte Gleichnisse Jesu aus dem Thomas-Evangelium', in W. Eltester (ed.), *Judentum, Urchristentum, Kirche* (Berlin 1964), p.

217, that the opening phrase is a gnostic modification of 'The kingdom of heaven is like'.

5. F. F. Bruce suggested that the big fish is 'either the true gnostic, whom Christ chooses above all others, or the true knowledge for which the gnostic abandons everything else' (Bruce, *Origins*, p. 116); but this is to presuppose that *Thomas* is gnostic through and through.

6. The Jesus Seminar considered that *Thomas* has preserved the form of this parable that is closest to the original (Funk, *Five Gospels*, p. 478).

7. See C. C. Torrey, *Our Translated Gospels* (Harper & Bros 1936), pp. 7f.; Black, *Aramaic Approach*, p. 162; Taylor, *The Gospel according to St Mark* (Macmillan 1953), p. 252; Cranfield, *Mark*, p. 149.

8. Montefiore and Turner, *Thomas*, p. 34, hold the gnostic view. Compare A. J. B. Higgins, 'Non-gnostic sayings in the Gospel of Thomas', in *Novum Testamentum* 4 (1960), p. 296.

9. An entirely different interpretation of this parable sees the reference to undressing as alluding to Christian baptism and concludes that the parable in its present form reflects theological concerns that did not originate with Jesus. See Funk, *Five Gospels*, p. 485.

10. See Jeremias, *Parables*, p. 49.

11. See A. Olrik, 'Epic Laws of Folk Narrative' in A. Dundes (ed.), *The Study of Folklore* (Prentice-Hall 1965), pp. 133f.; Crossan, *Four Other Gospels*, p. 41, suggests that the second excuse has been added in *Thomas*, while Patterson (*Thomas and Jesus*, p. 78, note 305) argues for the first as the extra one.

12. There is a detailed comparison of the *Thomas* version with those in the synoptic gospels in my article in *Expository Times* 98 (1986/7), pp. 104–7. For a sermon on the same parable, see *Expository Times* 97 (1985/6), pp. 145–7: 'Murder amongst the Vines!'

13. See Dodd, *Parables*, p. 129.

14. J. A. T. Robinson argued from his examination of this version of the parable that *Thomas* appears to go back to a tradition independent of our synoptic gospels (Robinson, *Trust?* pp. 55–61).

15. This is the view of Jeremias, *Parables*, p. 199: 'If Matthew makes the merchant a dealer in pearls, that is surely a secondary feature, since it anticipates the element of surprise.'

16. Again, Jeremias (*Parables*, p. 200) regards this as the original version. He believes that Matthew has heightened the meaning under the influence of the previous verse, Matthew 13.44, where we read that the farmer sold everything that he had in order to be able to buy the field containing the hidden treasure. J. D. M. Derrett (*Law in the New Testament*, Darton, Longman & Todd 1970, p. 13, note 4) agrees that the version in *Thomas* is attractive since *Thomas* makes the servant sell all his merchandise, not all he had. On the other hand, B. Dehandschutter in 'Parabole de la Perle et L'Évangile

selon Thomas', in *Ephemerides Theologicae* 55 (1979), pp. 243–65, argues that the context of *Thomas* 76 and its wording, in comparison with Matthew 13.45–46, reflects the gnostic character of the document as a whole. *Thomas* 76 accentuates the sacrifice demanded in finding the treasure (the kingdom or *gnosis*). He maintains that the non-gnostic encratite interpretation is difficult to sustain.

17. Montefiore takes this change as showing *Thomas's* individualistic conception of the kingdom as the spiritual state of the individual gnostic (Montefiore and Turner, *Thomas*, p. 76).

18. See Jeremias, *Parables*, p. 101.

19. Grant and Freedman (*Secret Sayings*, p. 176) declare that the change of subject shows *Thomas's* emphasis on the action of the gnostic, not on the work of God. A. J. B. Higgins in 'Non-Gnostic Sayings in the Gospel of Thomas', in *Novum Testamentum* (1960), p. 301, declares that Grant and Freedman, 'in their search for the ubiquitous gnostic, are perhaps too subtle in seeing any real significance in the comparison of the kingdom with a woman instead of with leaven, as in the synoptics.'

20. Compare R. Doran, 'A Complex of Parables: GTh 96–98', in *Novum Testamentum* 29 (1987), p. 348: 'The emphasis in Thomas' telling is on the practical know-how of the good cook.' See also my commentary in *Third Way* 12 (October 1989), p. 21: 'A new recipe for bread'. I disagree with the conclusion of the Jesus Seminar that the explicit contrast between a little leaven and large loaves has been introduced into the parable and is alien to the genuine parables of Jesus (Funk, *Five Gospels*, p. 523). This contrast in *Thomas* 96 is similar to others in *Thomas* 8 (9.1) and *Thomas* 20 (9.3).

21. Marshall, *Luke*, p. 561.

22. This is the view of Quispel, who writes (*Tatian and Thomas*, p. 52): 'Here we have one of those cases where Thomas is not only independent of the canonical gospels, but also seems to have preserved a tradition that is nearer to the source.'

23. In the Jesus Seminar, some considered it to be a parody of the story of Elijah and the widow at Zarephath, whose jar of meal did not become empty (1 Kings 17.8–16). Others felt that it might be authentic in spite of the fact that it does not occur in any of the canonical gospels (Funk, *Five Gospels*, p. 524).

24. See Quispel, 'The Gospel of Thomas and the New Testament', in *Vigiliae Christianae* 11 (1957), p. 205.

25. R. Doran, 'A Complex of Parables: GTh 96–98', pp. 351f. (see note 20).

26. 'The sheer violence and scandal of the image of the assassin suggests that it might well have originated with Jesus. It is unlikely that the early Christian community would have invented and have attributed such a story to Jesus since its imagery is so contrary to

the irenic and honorific images, such as the good shepherd, they customarily used for him' (Funk, *Five Gospels*, p. 524).

27. See Kloppenberg, *Q Parallels*, pp. 174f.

28. This is different from the view taken by Marshall, *Luke*, p. 600, who declares that *Thomas* 107 'draws a gnostic lesson from it, by making the shepherd love the lost sheep, which was the biggest in the flock, more than the others.'

29. Compare W. L. Petersen in 'The Parable of the Lost Sheep in the Gospel of Thomas and the Synoptic Gospels', in *Novum Testamentum* 23 (1981), pp. 128–47.

30. For example, E. Haenchen, *Die Botschaft des Thomas-Evangeliums* (Alfred Töpelmann 1961), p. 47; N. Perrin, *Rediscovering the Teaching of Jesus* (SCM 1967), p. 88: 'As it stands in Thomas, the parable teaches the gnostic conception that most men have no idea what treasure they have within themselves and so not everyone finds the treasure in his field = discovers the divine self within.'

31. R. M. Grant, 'Notes on the Gospel of Thomas', in *Vigiliae Christianae* 13 (1959), p. 170.

32. H. H. McArthur (ed.), *New Testament Sidelights: Essays in Honor of Alexander Converse Purdy* (The Hartford Seminary Foundation Press 1960), p. 54.

33. For example, Schrage, *Thomas*, p. 118; B. D. Chilton, 'The Gospel according to Thomas as a Source of Jesus' Teaching', in D. Wenham (ed.), *Gospel Perspectives – vol. 5: The Jesus Tradition outside the Gospels* (JSOT 1985), p. 157.

34. See A. L. Nations, *A Critical Study of the Coptic Gospel according to Thomas* (Nashville, Tennesee: PhD Thesis 1960), p. 153.

35. It is translated thus in Guillaumont, *Thomas*, p. 33, as well as in Layton, *Nag Hammadi*, p. 75.

36. See Funk, *Five Gospels*, p. 506; Bruce, *Origins*, p. 136; Grant, *Secret Sayings*, p. 156.

37. The translation of Thomas Lambdin (Layton, *Nag Hammadi*, p. 79) is similar to mine and would support this interpretation of the beatitude.

38. Thomas Lambdin (Layton, *Nag Hammadi*, p. 81) translates: 'Blessed are the hungry, for the belly of him who desires will be filled.'

39. Montefiore and Turner, *Thomas*, pp. 35, 38 and 96.

Chapter Ten

1. This is the view of Haenchen (*Botschaft*, p. 35) but contrary to Gärtner (*Theology*, pp. 98ff.) and to Stanton (*Jesus*, p. 133), who maintains that the sayings in *Thomas* 'are meant to be understood as logia of the risen Jesus and not of Jesus of Nazareth. . . . In other gnostic documents where Jesus speaks to his disciples, it is as the

risen Jesus during the post-resurrection period, and this is the case here.'

2. In a very detailed lexicographical study in *Journal of Theological Studies* 30 (1979), pp. 15–36, A. C. Thiselton shows that the Greek word has this meaning in the writings of Philo and Josephus.

3. This could be the meaning of the words of Papias regarding Mark quoted by Eusebius 3.39.16: 'Mark, when he had become the interpreter of Peter, wrote down accurately what he remembered of the things said and done by the Lord.' See Cranfield, *Mark*, pp. 3f.

4. The Coptic word translated here as 'all things' (see also *Thomas* 67 – 10.9 and *Thomas* 77 – 11.17) occurs in the Sahidic Coptic New Testament in four places (Romans 11.36; 1 Corinthians 8.6; Philippians 3.21; Hebrews 2.10) as the equivalent of Greek words meaning 'all things'. Neither in the New Testament nor in *Thomas* should it be rendered 'the All' as most people do in *Thomas* 2, 67 and 77, since that immediately suggests the gnostic idea of the whole of cosmic reality. This was the (in my view) mistaken conclusion of the members of the Jesus Seminar (see Funk, *Five Gospels*, p. 512).

5. A compound verb is used in Matthew 16.24 and Mark 8.34 with the same meaning.

6. See O. Cullman, 'The Gospel of Thomas and the Problem of the Age of the Tradition contained therein', in *Interpretation* 16 (1962), p. 429.

7. See note 4 above, on *Thomas* 2 (10.2).

8. This is an attempt to render the Coptic first habitude tense, which is not usually found as a translation of the Greek future.

9. Compare *Thomas* 35 (12.16), *Thomas* 41 (12.19), *Thomas* 54 (9.20), *Thomas* 73 (12.26).

10. The form of the verb in *Thomas* 34 ('are in the habit of falling') seems to indicate a source more primitive than the synoptic gospels is being used and also that the Coptic text is not a translation from a Greek original. Compare the view of A. L. Nations (see chapter 9, note 34) p. 150.

11. See Hunter, *Design*, pp. 59–75.

12. The first part of the reply of Jesus should probably have been inserted into *Thomas* 5 (10.32). The answer to the questions about the three pious acts would then come in *Thomas* 14 (10.18). Compare Davies, *Thomas*, pp. 153ff.

13. The negative form occurs in various other places including Acts 15.20, 29 in Codex Bezae; *Didache* 1.2; Babylonian Talmud, Shabbat 31a; and sentences of the Syriac Menander (third century AD).

14. Compare K. Grobel, 'How Gnostic is the Gospel of Thomas?', in *New Testament Studies* 8 (1961/2), pp. 367–73, who declares that 'Thomas has eliminated the allegedly gnostic trademark' and that

the reversal in order of clauses suggests 'that Thomas is here more likely dependent upon oral tradition than written'.

15. H. L. Strack and P. Billerbeck, *Kommentar zum Neuen Testament aus Talmud und Midrash* (München: C. H. Beck 1922–61), vol. 1: 4.1.35.

16. See Dodd, *Parables*, pp. 34–110; Hunter, *Work and Words*, pp. 90–100.

17. Grant, *Secret Sayings*, p. 108; compare J. D. G. Dunn, *Unity and Diversity in the New Testament* (SCM 1977), p. 286: 'Thomas lacks any eschatological interest whatsoever [changed in revised edition of 1990 to 'In Thomas eschatological interest is almost exclusively absent'] and the synoptic-like material which it has preserved has been thoroughly de-eschatologized.' Even Koester (Robinson and Koester, *Trajectories*, p. 172) declares: 'These (kingdom) sayings almost always show a tendency to emphasize the presence of the kingdom for the believer rather than its future coming. But it is very questionable whether such eschatology of the kingdom is a later gnostic spiritualization of early Christian apocalyptic expectation or rather an interpretation and elaboration of Jesus' most original proclamation.'

18. Koester, (Robinson and Koester, *Trajectories*, p. 172) states: 'The *Gospel of Thomas* does not reveal any acquaintance with either the synoptic apocalypse or Q's Son of man expectation.' There is only one saying in which the phrase 'Son of man' occurs (*Thomas* 86 – 11.8).

19. It is not so obvious to me, as it was to Jeremias (*Unknown Sayings*, p. 12, note 6), that 'this saying is obviously of a gnostic character. It makes Jesus the mouthpiece of the common gnostic doctrine that peace is already a present possibility for those who have received knowledge.'

20. Compare Jeremias, *Parables*, p. 221, note 66.

Chapter Eleven

1. See R. T. Herford, *Christianity in Talmud and Midrash* (Williams & Norgate 1903), pp. 35–40; J. Klausner, *Jesus of Nazareth: his Life, Times and Teaching* trans. N. Danby (Allen & Unwin 1929), pp. 18–24; M. W. Meyer, 'Making Mary Male: the Categories "Male" and "Female" in the Gospel of Thomas', in *New Testament Studies* 31 (1985), pp. 554–70.

2. Many years ago, E. Wendling in *Die Entstehung des Marcus Evangeliums* (Mohr 1908, pp. 53–6) suggested that the saying found at Oxyrhynchus was more primitive than that in the canonical gospels. Bultmann in *History of the Synoptic Tradition* (Blackwell 1963, p. 31) agreed with him: 'It is hardly likely that the double proverb has grown out of Mark 6.1–6. The reverse is on the other hand probable.'

3. S. J. Noorda in 'Classical and Rabbinical Parallels to an alleged Saying of Jesus', in J. Delobel (ed.), *Logia: Les Paroles de Jésus – the Sayings of Jesus* (Leuven University Press 1982), pp. 459–67, tabulates twenty-five parallels referred to in the history of interpretation.

4. See, for example, Stanton, *Jesus*, pp. 132f.: 'The addition of "and to rest" may be a deliberate alteration in a gnostic direction.' Yet Stanton proceeds: 'The logion is merely a statement about the Son of Man; an application to the disciple or gnostic is not made explicit.' Compare, A. J. B. Higgins, 'Non-Gnostic Sayings in the Gospel of Thomas', in *Novum Testamentum* 4 (1960), p. 300; 'Possibly the addition of rest is a gnostic addition.' See also Montefiore and Turner, p. 54, where it is stated that the parable of the foxes and the birds 'refers to the true "rest" of the gnostic'.

5. See H. K. McArthur, *New Testament Sidelights* (Hartford Seminary Foundation Press 1960), p. 53, where it is stated that the version of the saying in *Thomas* 71 'underlines the overthrow of the old regime by Jesus, or at least this may be its intent'.

6. See Koester in Layton, *Rediscovery*, p. 246: 'Except for "lordship" instead of "burden" (Matthew 11.30), this shorter version could be more original than Matthew's. Signs of Matthew's editorial work are missing in *Thomas* 90.'

7. Ian Wilson (*Words of Jesus?* p. 62) regards *Thomas* 17 as being one of many sayings in *Thomas* that 'have the authority, simplicity and directness that we have come to associate with utterances genuinely attributable to Jesus. . . . Although this partly harks back to Isaiah 64.4, it has that extra twist typical of Jesus. And Paul in his first letter to the Corinthians seemed specifically to have heard this saying as an utterance from Jesus.' But Paul does not say that it is a word of the Lord. He declares: 'As it has been written'.

8. A. L. Nations (see chapter 9, note 34) suggests a translation similar to mine. The Jesus Seminar came to the conclusion that the Coptic version of the saying is probably corrupt, the result of a mistranslation from a Greek original (see Funk, *Five Gospels*, p. 489). Patterson (*Thomas and Jesus*, p. 153) draws attention to a suggested reconstruction of the Coptic text which could be rendered: 'Where there are [three], they are (without God), and where there is but [a single one], I say I am with [him].'

9. See 10.2 and chapter 10 note 4 for the translation of the Coptic word meaning 'all things'.

10. Compare Hunter, *Teaching and Preaching*, p. 32: 'Notice the two kinds of work mentioned. Lifting stones and splitting wood may sound like the dreariest kind of labour and the least spiritual. No, says Jesus, even such labour may be transfigured by a hidden glory. As in Matthew 18.20 he promises his presence to the two or three

who gather in his name, so here he assures it to the humble toiler who believes in him. What seems like cheerless drudgery may be lustred by the presence of the Saviour.'

Chapter Twelve

1. See B. D. Chilton, 'The Gospel according to Thomas as a Source of Jesus' Teaching', in D. Wenham (ed.), *Gospel Perspectives – vol. 5: The Jesus Tradition outside the Gospels* (JSOT 1985), pp. 155–75.
2. See W. A. Meeks, 'The Image of the Androgynous: some uses of a symbol in earliest Christianity', in *History of Religions* 13 (1973/4), p. 183: 'There can be little doubt that the "taking off" and "putting on" is first of all an interpretation of the act of disrobing, which must have preceded baptism, and of the dressing afterward. By being taken up into the symbolic language these simple procedures become ritual acts.' Compare J. Z. Smith, *Map is not Territory: Studies in the History of Religions* (Brill 1978), p. 8: 'That which definitely places logion 37 within the context of the Christian rite of baptism is the injunction to tread upon one's garments.'
3. Ephraem (about AD 306–73) was a voluminous Syrian biblical exegete and ecclesiastical writer, whose writings were mostly in verse. He wrote in Syriac.
4. W. E. Crum, *A Coptic Dictionary* (Clarendon Press 1939, 1972) 218b, gives the meaning of the Coptic verb as 'be great' but also lists as one of its occurrences in the Coptic New Testament Matthew 23.5, where it is the equivalent of the Greek verb meaning 'make great'. The scribes and Pharisees are denounced for 'making great' the tassels on their robes. The Greek verb also occurs elsewhere with the significance of 'declare great', 'extol', 'magnify'; for example, Luke 1.47; Acts 5.13; 2 Corinthians 10.46.
5. It is not so obvious to me, as it was to the Jesus Seminar (see Funk, *Five Gospels*, p. 487), that this saying is clearly a gnostic formulation.
6. Quispel (*Tatian and Thomas*, pp. 79f.) has argued that this form of the saying is (1) very Semitic; (2) presupposed in the *Didache* and in the *Testaments of the Twelve Patriarchs*; (3) found in the Persian Diatessaron. 'This clearly shows that, beside the canonical version, the saying of Jesus was current in certain Jewish quarters of Christianity in a different wording and at a very early date.'
7. See G. Quispel, 'Some Remarks on the Gospel of Thomas', in *New Testament Studies* 5 (1985/9), p. 285.
8. T. W. Manson, *The Sayings of Jesus* (SCM 1937, 1949), pp. 152f.; Jeremias, *Parables*, p. 109; Funk, *Five Gospels*, p. 492: 'Since the original context has been lost in both Matthew and Thomas, we cannot determine what it meant on the lips of Jesus.'
9. This is the view of Haenchen, *Botschaft*, p. 41. It is hardly likely to be a gnostic expansion of a synoptic saying, as, for example, M.

Marcovich, *Studies in Graeco-Roman Religions and Gnosticism* (Brill 1988), p. 57: 'The disciples of the gnostic Jesus are expected to hear canonical sayings in one ear and their gnostic interpretation in the other.'

10. See Jeremias, *Parables*, p. 120; Montefiore and Turner, *Thomas*, p. 58.

11. This is also the view of the Jesus Seminar. See Funk, *Five Gospels*, p. 493.

12. See commentary on *Thomas* 34 (10.14) and chapter 10, note 10; Patterson, *Thomas and Jesus*, p. 37.

13. Jeremias (*Unknown Sayings*, p. 114) thought that this saying was an earlier form of the Arabic bridge saying (17.30), whose authenticity he doubted. On the other hand, some members of the Jesus Seminar felt that it cohered with other sayings attributed to Jesus in which he advocates a mendicant or countercultural lifestyle and were prepared to regard it as being genuine, although other members were inclined to view it as reflecting patterns of social behaviour in community, presumably in Edessa in Syria (Funk, *Five Gospels*, p. 496). Patterson (*Thomas and Jesus*, pp. 128–31) discusses in detail various other suggested versions, including 'Be wanderers' and 'Be Hebrews', the latter based on the similarity of the Hebrew words for 'wanderer' and 'Hebrews'. Quispel ('Gnosticism in the New Testament', in J. P. Hyatt (ed.), *The Bible in Modern Scholarship*, Abingdon Press 1965, p. 254) suggested 'Become wanderers' and continued: 'In obedience to this commandment the Syrian ascetics kept wandering until the fourth century.'

14. Jeremias, *Parables*, p. 104; Schrage, p. 112; Patterson (*Thomas and Jesus*, p. 102) argues against the dependence of *Thomas* on Luke from the different positions and formulations of the saying in the two documents.

15. The second part of this saying is usually translated as, 'but there is nothing in the well'. However, Origen in his work *Against Celsus* 8.15 quotes from an anti-Christian document written about AD 178: 'In one place in the heavenly dialogue they speak these words: "If the Son of God is mightier and the Son of man is his Lord how is it that many are round the well and no one goes into it?" ' Origen did not know from where Celsus got this. See H. Chadwick, *Contra Celsum* (Cambridge University Press 1953, 1980), pp. 462f.; Grant, *Secret Sayings*, p. 166.

16. In *Didache* 9.5, the first clause is used with reference to the Eucharist.

17. According to Grant, *Secret Sayings*, p. 178, *Thomas* relegates what belongs to Caesar and to God to a place of inferiority, compared with the inner man, who belongs to Jesus. However, this seems to be reading gnosticism into the saying.

18. This is the view of Montefiore and Turner, *Thomas*, p. 89.

19. See Crossan, *Four Other Gospels*, pp. 77–87.

20. Compare Jeremias (*Unknown Sayings*, pp. 66–73), who is in no doubt either about its authenticity or about the identity of Origen's source as being the *Gospel of Thomas*. He also draws attention to the fact that the saying is quoted in Greek by Didymus the Blind (about AD 313–98), who also found it in a Greek edition of the *Gospel of Thomas*.

Chapter Thirteen

1. See Hennecke, vol. 1, pp. 363–417, 437–44.
2. Eusebius, *Church History* 1.13; W. Cureton, *Ancient Syriac Documents relative to the earliest establishment of Christianity in Edessa* (Williams & Norgate 1864); J. B. Segal, *Edessa and Haran* (London School of Oriental and African Studies 1963).
3. See L. W. Barnard, 'The Origins and Emergence of the Church in Edessa during the first two centuries AD', in *Vigiliae Christianae* 22 (1968), pp. 162–75; J. L. Gardner (ed.), *Atlas of the Bible* (Reader's Digest 1983), p. 165.

Chapter Fourteen

1. Eusebius, *Church History*, 6.12.2–6; Hennecke, vol. 1, pp. 179–87; Crossan, *Four Other Gospels*, pp. 125–35.
2. This does not necessarily imply a docetic view of Jesus, as F. F. Bruce seemed to suggest: 'The cry of dereliction is reproduced in a form which suggests that, at that moment, his divine power left the bodily shell in which it had taken up temporary residence' (Bruce, *Origins*, p. 93).
3. Hennecke, vol. 2, pp. 259–322.
4. This is one of the sayings whose authenticity, according to Joachim Jeremias, admits of serious consideration (Jeremias, *Unknown Sayings*, pp. 90–2).
5. Compare Dunkerley, *Beyond Gospels*, p. 115: 'That Jesus often spoke in enigmas to arrest attention and arouse thought seems certain from the gospels, and this is a striking example of that method of teaching.'
6. According to Wesley Isenberg (Layton, *Nag Hammadi*, p. 131; Robinson, *Nag Hammadi*, p. 131), the *Gospel of Philip* makes an important contribution to our rather limited knowledge of gnostic sacramental theology and practice.
7. See R. McL. Wilson, *The Gospel of Philip* (Mowbray 1962) [Wilson, *Philip*], p. 83.
8. Wilson, *Philip*, p. 92; Gärtner, *Theology*, p. 206.
9. Wilson, *Philip*, p. 114.
10. Wilson, *Philip*, pp. 158–60, gives a detailed account of various interpretations of this saying, including the suggestion that the gnostic can laugh because he despises the world and regards it as a

joke. However, it is not at all clear that there is a gnostic reference here.

Chapter Fifteen

1. Hennecke, vol. 1, pp. 117–78.
2. William Barclay, *The New Testament* (Collins 1968), vol. 1, p. 67.
3. Jeremias (*Unknown Sayings*, pp. 94–6), while considering the case for the originality and independence of this saying as borderline, nevertheless declares that the language and subject matter have a definite Palestinian colouring.
4. Dunkerley (*Beyond Gospels*, p. 106) believes that, if this is an alternative account of the synoptic incident, 'then it certainly does appear to have certain primitive touches which it is worth preserving'. Compare Jeremias (*Unknown Sayings*, pp. 44–7), who declares that the Palestinian colouring is beyond all question and that several other features make it difficult to regard the story as completely worthless.
5. Compare Jeremias (*Unknown Sayings*, pp. 92–4), who concludes: 'Here is the acid test of true discipleship. A true disciple is happy only when every barrier between himself and his brother has been broken down.' See also W. G. Morrice, *We Joy in God* (SPCK 1977), pp. 39–42, for further comment on love and joy as two parts of the harvest of the Spirit referred to by Paul in Galatians 5.22f.

Chapter Sixteen

1. Jeremias, *Unknown Sayings*, pp. 76f.
2. According to Jeremias (*Unknown Sayings*, p. 84), many scholars have concluded that Justin wrongly attributed this saying to Jesus. However, the fact that it occurs in so many places including three independent witnesses – Justin Martyr (second century), Cyprian (third century) and the fourth-century Syrian *Book of Stages* (see 16.26) – seems to have persuaded Jeremias to regard it as genuine, a conclusion endorsed by Otfried Hofius (*Jesusworte*, p. 373). Compare Hunter, *Teaching and Preaching*, pp. 31f.: 'Our Lord is looking away to the great Day. When he comes in glory, he will not go peering into the past; he will take men and judge them as he finds them. And blessed are those whom he will find abounding in the work of the Lord.'
3. Hofius (*Jesusworte*, p. 375) agrees with the conclusion of Jeremias (*Unknown Sayings*, pp. 98–100) that the possibility of this being an independent and authentic saying of Jesus remains as being thoroughly worthy of consideration.
4. According to Jeremias (*Unknown Sayings*, p. 101), Alfred Resch (**18.4**, and chapter 18 note 5) discovered thirty-seven quotations and twenty allusions, though Smith (*Unwritten Sayings*, p. 106) says

that Resch collected no fewer than sixty-nine quotations. Compare Hunter, *Teaching and Preaching*, p. 29, who writes that this 'unfamiliar saying addressed to disciples is quoted so frequently in early Christian writings that its genuineness is beyond dispute'.

5. Hunter, *Teaching and Preaching*, pp. 29f.; Jackson, *Agrapha*, pp. 32–4; Jeremias, *Unknown Sayings*, pp. 100–4; Smith, *Unwritten Sayings*, pp. 105–14.

6. Jackson (*Agrapha*, p. 52) calls attention to the fact that Ropes (*Die Sprüche*, pp. 123f.) calls this a beautiful saying that is worthy of a place in the gospel.

7. Jeremias (*Unknown Sayings*, p. 21, note 8) points out that the *Liber Graduum* contains a large number of *agrapha* which have never received a thorough investigation and analysis.

8. Jeremias (*Unknown Sayings*, p. 86) regards this form of the saying as being the older version on the grounds that it is not yet coloured by the Church's Christology, that it speaks only of the irruption of the End and what it will mean for those who are still alive, and that it contains the reverential passive.

9. Marshall, *Luke*, p. 594.

10. Jeremias, *Unknown Sayings*, p. 35. 'Such transferences . . . were based on serious theological grounds. In the words of the witnesses, both of the Old Covenant and of the New, the Church hears the voice of the pre-existent and exalted Lord.'

Chapter Seventeen

1. See Parrinder, *Quran*.

2. Dunkerley, *Beyond Gospels*, p. 145.

3. D. S. Margoliouth, 'Christ in Islam', in *Expository Times* 5 (1893/4), pp. 59, 107, 177f., 503f., 561. [Margoliouth]

4. Ropes, *Agrapha*.

5. Michael Asin et Palacios, 'Logia et Agrapha Domini Jesu apud Moslemicos Scriptores, asceticos praesertim, usitata collegit, vertit, notis instruxit', in *Patrologia Orientalis* 13, no. 3 (Paris 1919) and 19, no. 4 (Paris 1925/6). [Asin]

6. Robson, *Christ in Islam*.

7. Dunkerley, *Beyond Gospels*; Roderic Dunkerley, 'The Muhammedan Agrapha', in *Expository Times* 39 (1927/8), pp. 167ff., 230ff.

8. Dunkerley (*Beyond Gospels*, p. 152) quotes A. Mingana as remarking about the Arabic sayings generally: 'To say that they have simply been invented by the writers who quoted them is an hypothesis which does not seem to be very attractive.' Dunkerley continues: 'Personally I take the view that genuine fragments are included even though we cannot reach any high degree of certainty about the identification of them' (p. 153).

9. Dunkerley, *Beyond Gospels*, pp. 152f.

10. Dunkerley (*Beyond Gospels*, p. 146) refers to this as 'one of the most beautiful stories told of Jesus in this literature'.
11. Jane Ellice Hopkins, *Autumn Swallows* (Macmillan 1883).
12. Smith, *Unwritten Sayings*, pp. 71–82; Dunkerley, *Beyond Gospels*, p. 146; Jeremias, *Unknown Sayings*, pp. 111–18.
13. Jeremias, *Unknown Sayings*, p. 117; Hunter (*Teaching and Preaching*, p. 25) notes that Jeremias doubts its authenticity but points out that the saying can be traced back before the time of Mohammed and notes how like its teaching is to Jesus' parable of the rich fool.
14. Smith, *Unwritten Sayings*, pp. 74–9.

Chapter Eighteen
1. William Barclay, Review of Dunkerley, *Beyond Gospels* in *Expository Times* 69 (1957/8), p. 318.
2. Compare Jeremias, *Unknown Sayings*, p. 120: 'The extra-canonical literature, taken as a whole, manifests a surprising poverty. The bulk of it is legendary, and bears the clear mark of forgery. Only here and there, amid a mass of worthless rubbish, do we come across a priceless jewel. The range of material which is of any use to the historian is remarkably small.'
3. As we have already noted (8.3), the Coptic *Gospel of Thomas* contains 114 composite sayings but for the purposes of this book *Thomas* 22 has been divided into two parts (10.25; 10.26) as has *Thomas* 69 (9.23; 9.24), while *Thomas* 79 has been split into three (a, b and c), but only b and c are included (9.25; 9.26) since 79a is a beatitude on Jesus' mother on the lips of a woman from the crowd.
4. Of the 114 sayings in *Thomas*, 84 have echoes in the New Testament (see Table 1 – 8.3), but only 54 of these provide parallels that can be compared with sayings of Jesus in the canonical gospels.
5. Compare Stanton, *Gospel Truth?* p. 134: 'A thorough search of all early Christian writings for possible references to words of Jesus confirms the value of the canonical Gospels as evidence for the life and teaching of Jesus. . . . We have looked in several fascinating nooks and crannies. For the historian every phrase from outside the Gospels is gold, but there isn't much of it.'
6. Alfred Resch, *Agrapha: Aussercanonische Schriftfragmente* (Hinrich 1906). Resch had his own theory concerning the origin of the synoptic gospels based on his study of the *agrapha*. He believed that behind Matthew, Mark and Luke lay an original collection of sayings composed by Matthew in Hebrew, which was also used by Paul and John. From this were also derived all the *agrapha*. This solution of the synoptic problem was generally rejected.
7. Ropes, *Die Sprüche*.
8. Jackson, *Agrapha*.
9. Ropes, *Agrapha*.

10. Smith, *Unwritten Sayings*, p. 18.
11. Jeremias, *Unknown Sayings*, pp. 13, 42.
12. It would appear that Jeremias rejected another saying as well but he did not make absolutely clear which it was. He does consider in passing, and within the context of his examination of the Arabic bridge saying, *Thomas* 42 – 12.20: 'Become passers by'.
13. Jeremias, *Unknown Sayings*, pp. 120f.
14. Hunter, *Teaching and Preaching*, p. 26.
15. Hofius, *Jesusworte*.
16. Stroker, *Extracanonical Sayings*.
17. Wilson, *Words of Jesus?* p. 63.
18. James M. Robinson, *A New Quest of the Historical Jesus* (SCM 1959), p. 63.
19. Pagels, *Gnostic Gospels*.
20. See Meyer, *Thomas*, pp. 111–21.
21. See Davies, *Thomas*, pp. 100–6.
22. Funk, *Five Gospels*, p. xiv.

Suggestions for Further Reading

with short titles in square brackets [] for reference purposes

Baarda, T., *Early Transmission of Words of Jesus: Thomas, Tatian and the Text of the New Testament* (Boekhandel/Uitgeverij 1983) [Baarda, *Thomas, Tatian and Text*].

Black, Matthew, *An Aramaic Approach to the Gospels and Acts* (Clarendon Press 1946, 1967) [Black, *Aramaic Approach*].

Bruce, F. F., *Jesus and Christian Origins outside the New Testament* (Hodder & Stoughton 1974) [Bruce, *Origins*].

Cranfield, C. E. B., *The Gospel according to St Mark* (Cambridge University Press 1966) [Cranfield, *Mark*].

Crossan, John D., *Four Other Gospels: Shadows on the Contours of the Canon* (Harper & Row 1985) [Crossan, *Four Other Gospels*].

Crossan, John D., *Sayings Parallels: A Workbook for the Jesus Tradition* (Fortress Press 1986) [Crossan, *Parallels*].

Davies, Stevan L., *The Gospel of Thomas and Christian Wisdom* (Seabury Press 1983) [Davies, *Thomas*].

Dodd, C. H., *New Testament Studies* (Manchester University Press 1953) [Dodd, *Studies*].

Dodd, C. H., *The Parables of the Kingdom* (Nisbet 1935) [Dodd, *Parables*].

Dunkerley, Roderic, *Beyond the Gospels* (Penguin 1957) [Dunkerley, *Beyond Gospels*].

Elliott, J. K., *The Apocryphal Jesus: Legends of the Early Church* (Oxford University Press 1996).

Finegan, Jack, *Encountering New Testament Manuscripts* (SPCK 1975) [Finegan, *Manuscripts*].

Frend, William H. C., *The Rise of Christianity* (Darton, Longman & Todd 1984) [Frend, *Rise*].

Funk, Robert W., Roy W. Hoover, and the Jesus Seminar, *The Five Gospels: The Search for the Authentic Words of Jesus – New Translation and Commentary* (Macmillan 1995) [Funk, *Five Gospels*].

Gärtner, Bertil, *The Theology of the Gospel of Thomas* (Collins 1961) [Gärtner, *Theology*].

Grant, R. M. and D. N. Freedman, *The Secret Sayings of Jesus according to the Gospel of Thomas* (Collins 1960) [Grant, *Secret Sayings*].

Grenfell, B. P. and A. S. Hunt, *Oxyrhynchus Papyri* (Egyptian Exploration Fund 1898 and 1908).

Guillaumont, A., H.-Ch. Puech, G. Quispel, W. Till and Yassah 'Abd Al Masih, *The Gospel according to Thomas* (Brill and Collins 1959) [Guillaumont, *Thomas*].

Haenchen, E., *Die Botschaft des Thomas-Evangeliums* (Töpelman 1961) [Haenchen, *Botschaft*].

Hardy, E. R., *Christian Egypt: Church and People* (Oxford University Press 1952) [Hardy, *Egypt*].

Hedrick, C. W., *The Parables as Poetic Fictions* (Hendrickson 1994) [Hedrick, *Parables*].

Hennecke, E., *New Testament Apocrypha*. English translation edited by Robert McL. Wilson (SCM 1963) [Hennecke], revised edition (Clarke/Westminster/John Knox Press 1991).

Hofius, O., 'Unbekannte Jesusworte', in Peter Stuhlmacher (ed.), *Das Evangelium und die Evangelien: Vorträge vom Tübinger Symposium 1982* (Mohr 1983), pp. 355–81 [Hofius, *Jesusworte*].

Hunter, A. M., *According to John* (SCM 1968) [Hunter, *John*].

Hunter, A. M., *Design for Life* (SCM 1953) [Hunter, *Design*].

Hunter, A. M., *Interpreting the New Testament 1900–1950* (SCM 1951) [Hunter, *Interpreting*].

Hunter, A. M., *Introducing the New Testament* (SCM 1945, 1967) [Hunter, *Introducing*].

Hunter, A. M., *The Parables Then and Now* (SCM 1971) [Hunter, *Parables*].

Hunter, A. M., *Teaching and Preaching the New Testament* (SCM 1963) [Hunter, *Teaching and Preaching*].

Hunter, A. M., *The Work and Words of Jesus* (SCM 1950, 1973) [Hunter, *Work and Words*].

Jackson, Blomfield, *Twenty-Five Agrapha* (SPCK 1900) [Jackson, *Agrapha*].

Jenkinson, E. J., *The Unwritten Sayings of Jesus* (Epworth Press 1925) [Jenkinson, *Unwritten Sayings*].

Jeremias, Joachim, *The Eucharistic Words of Jesus* (Blackwell 1955) [Jeremias, *Eucharistic Words*].

Jeremias, Joachim, *The Parables of Jesus* (SCM 1963) [Jeremias, *Parables*].

Jeremias, Joachim, *Unknown Sayings of Jesus* (SPCK 1957, 1964) [Jeremias, *Unknown Sayings*].

Kloppenborg, John, *The Formation of Q* (Fortress Press 1987) [Kloppenborg, *Formation of Q*].

Kloppenborg, John, *Q Parallels: Synopsis, Critical Notes and Concordance* (Polebridge Press 1988) [Kloppenborg, *Q Parallels*].

Kloppenborg, John, Marvin Meyer, Stephen Patterson and Michael Steinhauser, *Q Thomas Reader* (Polebridge Press 1990) [Kloppenborg, *Q Thomas*].

Koester, Helmut, *Ancient Christian Gospels: Their History and Development* (SCM 1990) [Koester, *Ancient Gospels*].

Layton, Bentley (ed.), *Nag Hammadi Codex 2.2–7: volume one* (Brill 1989) [Layton, *Nag Hammadi*].

Layton, Bentley (ed.), *Rediscovery of Gnosticism* (Brill 1980) [Layton, *Rediscovery*].

Marshall. I. H., *The Gospel of Luke* (Paternoster 1978) [Marshall, *Luke*].

Meier, J. P., *A Marginal Jew* (Doubleday 1991) [Meyer, *Marginal*].

Ménard, Jacques-É., *L'Évangile selon Thomas* (Brill 1975) [Ménard, *Thomas*].

Meyer, Marvin, *The Gospel of Thomas: the Hidden Sayings of Jesus.* Translation, with introduction, critical edition of the Coptic text and notes with an interpretation by Harold Bloom (Harper 1992) [Meyer, *Thomas*].

Milligan, George, *Here and There among the Papyri* (Hodder & Stoughton 1922) [Milligan, *Here and There*].

Montefiore, H. and H. E. W. Turner, *Thomas and the Evangelists* (SCM 1962) [Montefiore and Turner, *Thomas*].

Moulton, Harold K., *Papyrus, Parchment and Print* (Lutterworth 1967) [Moulton, *Papyrus*].

Moulton, James H., *From Egyptian Rubbish-Heaps* (Kelly 1916) [Moulton, *Rubbish Heaps*].

Murray, Robert, *Symbols of Church and Kingdom: a Study in Early Syriac Tradition* (Cambridge University Press 1975) [Murray, *Symbols*].

Pagels, Elaine, *The Gnostic Gospels* (Weidenfeld & Nicolson 1979) [Pagels, *Gnostic Gospels*].

Parrinder, George, *Jesus in the Quran* (Faber & Faber 1965) [Parrinder, *Quran*].

Patterson, Stephen J., *The Gospel of Thomas and Jesus* (Polebridge 1993) [Patterson, *Thomas and Jesus*].

Piper, Ronald A. (ed.), *The Gospel behind the Gospels: Current Studies on Q* (Brill 1995) [Piper, *Gospel behind Gospels*].

Quispel, G., *Tatian and the Gospel of Thomas* (Brill 1975) [Quispel, *Tatian and Thomas*].

Robinson, James M. (ed.), *The Nag Hammadi Library in English* (Harper & Row 1981) [Robinson, *Nag Hammadi*].

Robinson, James M. and Helmut Koester, *Trajectories through early Christianity* (Fortress 1971) [Robinson and Koester, *Trajectories*].

Robinson, John A. T., *Can we trust the New Testament?* (Mowbrays 1977) [Robinson, *Trust?*].

Robinson, John A. T., *The Priority of John* (SCM 1985) [Robinson, *Priority*].

Robinson, John A. T., *Redating the New Testament* (SCM 1976) [Robinson, *Redating*].

Robson, James, *Christ in Islam* (John Murray 1929) [Robson, *Christ in Islam*].

Ropes, J. H., 'Agrapha', in James Hastings, *A Dictionary of the Bible* (T. & T. Clark 1904), pp. 343f. [Ropes, *Agrapha*].

Ropes, J. H., *Die Sprüche Jesu die in den kanonischen Evangelium nicht überliefert sind: eine kriische Bearbeitung des von D. Alfred Resch gesammelten Materiels* (Texte und Untersuchungen 14.2 – 1896) [Ropes, *Die Sprüche*].

Sanders, P. and M. Davies, *Studying the Synoptic Gospels* (SCM 1989) [Sanders and Davies, *Synoptic Gospels*].

Schrage, Wolfgang, *Das Verhältnis des Thomas-Evangeliums zur Synoptischen Tradition und zu den Koptischen Evangelienübersetzungen* (Töpelmann 1964) [Schrage, *Thomas*].

Segal, J. B., *Edessa and Haran* (London School of Oriental and African Studies 1963).

Smith, David, *Unwritten Sayings of Jesus* (Hodder & Stoughton 1913) [Smith, *Unwritten Sayings*].

Stanton, Graham, *Gospel Truth? New Light on Jesus and the Gospels* (Harper Collins 1995) [Stanton, *Gospel Truth?*].

Stanton, Graham, *Jesus of Nazareth in New Testament Preaching* (Cambridge University Press 1974) [Stanton, *Jesus*].

Streeter, B. H., *The Four Gospels* (Macmillan 1924) [Streeter, *Four Gospels*].

Stroker, William D., *Extracanonical Sayings of Jesus* (Scholars 1989) [Stroker, *Extracanonical Sayings*].

Taylor, Vincent, *The Text of the New Testament* (Macmillan 1961) [Taylor, *Text*].

Tuckett, C., *Nag Hammadi and the Gospel Tradition* (T. & T. Clark 1986) [Tuckett, *Nag Hammadi*].

Tuckett, C., *Reading the New Testament* (SPCK 1987) [Tuckett, *Reading*].

Veilleux, Armand, *Pachomian Koinonia* (Cistercian Publications 1980).

Wand, J. W. C., *A History of the Early Church* (Methuen 1937, 1949) [Wand, *History*].

Wilson, Ian, *Are these the Words of Jesus? Dramatic Evidence from beyond the New Testament* (Lennard Publishing 1990) [Wilson, *Words of Jesus?*].

Wilson, Robert McL., 'Nag Hammadi and the New Testament' in *New Testament Studies* 28 (1982), pp. 289–302 [Wilson, *Nag Hammadi*].

Wilson, Robert McL., *Studies in the Gospel of Thomas* (Mowbray 1960) [Wilson, *Studies in Thomas*].

Index of Biblical and Early Christian Sources

EARLY CHRISTIAN SOURCES

Thomas, Gospel of: 6, 9, 13–16, 22–4, 41, 56, 61–140

[Main reference given first in bold print]

Index of Authors and Subjects